MW00476056

Living the Dream

John Ford Sr.

North
Country
Press

Copyright © 2018 by John Ford Sr.

All rights reserved. No part of this book may be reproduced or transmitted in any form or by any means without written permission of the author.

ISBN 978-1-943424-44-3

Library of Congress Control Number: 2018963557

Cover design by Emily Newell

North Country Press
Unity, Maine

Foreword

"What do you want to be when you grow up?" If you are a parent or a grandparent, this is a natural question to put to a young person that you care about and wish good things for. On the other hand, if you are an early teenager plagued with uncertainty or self-doubt about life's choices and which path to take, this can be a question that some young people would just as soon not answer, or simply walk away from.

This is a fascinating subject for most people. The truth is that most of us, especially those of us who grew up in the 50s, didn't have a clue as a teenager what we wanted to do for work. Some of us were simply pushed along by circumstances, luck and twists of fate. Trial and error helped some of us to find useful and rewarding work; still others did what they had to do and sometimes spent a lifetime at work they really didn't enjoy or find fulfilling.

Blessed are those few among us who knew positively and absolutely, at a very young age, what they wanted to be when they grew up. John Ford, who wrote this book and a number of others, is one of those individuals. Not only did he know as a tyke that he wanted to be a Maine Game Warden, he, indeed, became one. And it became his life and a calling. "Living the Dream" is a perfect title for John's fourth book, for that is what he did.

John has been writing a monthly column for my publication, the Northwoods Sporting Journal, for many years now. His work is always humorous and fun. More than that, though, it is uplifting, just like John is as a person. Somewhere along the way, John and I became friends. His gift goes far beyond his commendable capacity to resurrect compelling stories from his old Warden diaries. His true gift is simply his outlook, the way he looks at life. To see other people and your own life through a prism that filters out the dark side of the human condition and sees the good and the funny side of life so often and so consistently is noteworthy – and this attribute lends itself to enjoyable books and heartwarming stories.

In "Living the Dream" John recounts his childhood life when his mother took in injured animals and nursed them to recovery for release again into the wilds. From an owl named "Hooty" to a raccoon named "Tater-Bug" and other creatures large and small, this was a special time in his young life, living in what he describes as a wildlife menagerie. He also recounts the many game wardens who set examples and inspired his vocational choosing, not the least of whom was his stepfather, Vernon Walker, who was a Maine Warden.

John includes in his book some of the more interesting trapping cases that he worked on and how much he had to learn about the sport. He says, "Once I got into it and understood the game, I then had the patience to sit for days in order to build a case, and how often times the courts never considered the time invested in developing a case. He includes photos with many of the incidents. Then he writes about the wild critters that he and his wife, Judy, raised, the characters they dealt with, and the memories associated with them. As we learn from all of John's books – this one included – he believed deeply that, on the job, integrity and fairness mattered. He prided himself on developing a lasting relationship with the public and depending upon informants. Keeping their information safe and secure so as not to damage their own reputations.

Above all, in "Living the Dream" John's natural gift for always finding a vein of humor, even at his own expense, is apparent throughout. In one of John's earlier books, John Marsh, a friend of John's and a well-known Maine Warden in his own right, suggests that John's "comedy was kind of a cover-up for the many stresses associated with being a game warden."

It's hard to see John as a cover-up artist, but if there is any truth to Marsh's observation, we can all take a life lesson from

John Ford, the man and the storyteller. Congratulations on another wonderful book, my friend. Thanks for living the dream, and for sharing it with us all.

V. Paul Reynolds, Editor
Northwoods Sporting Journal

Preface

In the following pages I hope to share with you my story. My story of pursuing and *"Living the Dream"* as a State of Maine Game Warden.

Follow along as I retrace the steps of my life's journey while fulfilling that dream of so long ago. Meet the many characters and enjoy some of the crazy antics that I had the opportunity to deal with over the 20 years of my great career. Including many of the wild animals that I loved being around. Share in the humor and the many interesting scenarios of what life on the beat as a District Game Warden was really like.

These real-life incidents were recorded directly from my daily diaries. Diaries that I kept during my great career. I owe the fact that I kept those diaries to my mentor and stepfather, Retired Warden Vernon Walker.

Verne was instrumental in helping this young warden starting out in his new career with welcomed advice and so many wise words of wisdom that I found to be priceless – the suggestion of keeping a diary being one of them. Verne wisely stated, "You want to keep a diary of the things that made this career the great career you thought it would be. If you fail to do it daily, the time will pass you by so quickly, you'll forget many of those things you wish you had jotted down as the time flies on by.

"Who knows, you might want to write a book someday. People really love hearing what life as a warden was really like," he enthusiastically stated. "I wish I'd kept those diaries back in my time!" he quipped.

I found his suggestion to be spot on, as the time out in the field did pass by way too quickly. Thank God, I followed his advice and faithfully kept those records of the many incidents and events I was involved in during that career.

I especially didn't want to recall those times when I was called upon to investigate the many tragedies, such as the hunting accidents, drownings, snowmobile fatalities, vehicle accidents and suicides, just to mention a few.

These were the things I wanted to purposely forget. There were those times when occasionally I got a chance to see the worst of my neighbors regarding fish and game and the brutality of the very animals we were entrusted to protect. But they were few and far between.

For the most part I've tried to list those things that kept me busy and those times that I found something humorous but not inclusive of those tragic duties we wardens all hated to perform. As I stated earlier, those tragic memories are the ones that I think any of us who have been there, would just as soon have forgotten.

In my other three books, *Suddenly the Cider Didn't Taste so Good, This Cider Still Tastes Funny, and Deer Diaries,* I related many of the real-life incidents of what the warden's job entailed.

In this book, I recall investigating many of the trapping cases that I'd neglected to tell in my other warden stories. I'd be the first to admit that when I started my illustrious career, trapping was something I knew very little about. Matter of fact, I knew nothing about it.

I was about as clued in on the trapping side of the business, and everything it entailed, as I'd been trying to play the piano at a highly publicized concert. In other words, I didn't have a clue about any of it, and I sure as hell couldn't play the piano!

Attempting to put a trapping case together required a lot of time, a lot of luck, and a whole lot of help from the very sportsmen I would be representing.

Before I get too far ahead of myself, let me share my story from the early beginning to the end. I hope you'll enjoy the moments as much as I did. As I write these memories today, I feel as though I am reliving that great career all over again.

My story begins with what life was like as a youngster, living in a house filled with a wide variety of wild critters. All of them in need of a little special care if they were to survive.

Being raised within that lifestyle is what prompted me to pursue the career I did. Eventually, that career brought me to where I was truly *"Living the Dream."*

Welcome to the Ford Menagerie

Growing up in Emery Mills, a small rural community located in York County, Maine, our home was sort of like living in a wildlife menagerie. And I loved every minute of it!

Unlike other kids my age – kids who had the normal house pets of a few cats and dogs, or a few farm animals roaming through their yards – we never knew from one minute to the next, just what wildlife critter would become the newest addition welcomed into our home.

Over the years there were several raccoon kits and a wide variety of other wild creatures that were eventually rehabilitated. They all were basically allowed to roam freely through our house.

For the most part they had been abandoned or orphaned critters. All of them in need of a caring and helping hand if they were going to survive.

By the grace of God, my mother possessed a special knack in providing that tender-loving-care these creatures needed. A care that many folks in the area depended upon her to provide, in order to give that helping hand that these animals so desperately required. She'd welcome any critter in distress, with the hopes of eventually releasing them back into the wilderness where they belonged, once they were capable of fending for themselves.

There were so many wild animals and birds that passed through the menagerie over the years it is difficult for me to remember them all. Most of them were facing a certain death sentence if they didn't get that special care she provided.

Like I stated earlier, many of them departed the menagerie weeks later after being fully rehabilitated and they were able to live a normal life out in the wild where they belonged.

There were fawns, an occasional bobcat, an otter or two, a few skunks, a couple of young woodchucks, porcupines, fox kits, several rabbits and squirrels, even a fisher, just to name a few of the many household guests passing through the doors of the so-called Ford Wildlife Menagerie.

All of these wild critters provided their fair share of memories. Priceless memories at that! Our menagerie also provided safe passage for several owls, hawks, ducks, partridge, and a variety of song birds that somehow made their way into the so-called sanctuary. I'm sure there were many other creatures that I've since forgotten.

A young male fisher named Fritzi was by far my all-time favorite. Fritzi was a story in himself. All of these wild animals needed some form of tender-loving-care if they were to survive.

Not all of them did! Whenever one died, it was a sad event for us personally. My mother simply hated losing a patient. It wasn't because she didn't try!

Anticipating some form of new wildlife critter roaming freely within our house became the normal way of life for this young fellow. Whether they had wings or feet, really made no difference! All of them were welcomed.

My mother's dedication and love for any wild beast or bird in distress was admirable to say the least. Never once did she ever refuse a critter. The raccoon kittens were by far the most frequent of the inhabitants. Their numbers were countless. Each one of them had their own little distinct personalities and they provided so many memories. Mostly all good!

My mother's willingness to assume the duties of Mother Nature to these little balls of yowling fur never faltered. She considered rescuing these wild animals and birds to be her calling. And so did the area game wardens, the animal control officers, the local police, or anyone else in the neighborhood who happened upon some wild creature in distress. Most of these young animals were considered as abandoned or, in some instances, the mother had unfortunately been killed.

Several of them were removed from vacant buildings where they were not welcomed by the owners – owners who were shocked to find a litter of baby raccoons had invaded their buildings, claiming the area as their own.

How could you not love having a critter like this to play with

In their haste to remedy their problems, once and for all, after scaring the mother away from her den, they seized the young kittens, packing them into a box or a crate and then, not knowing what to do with them, they simply called the local game warden or the local animal control officer to come to their rescue.

Meanwhile the mother raccoon, who had been forced to retreat from the sight, was watching from a distance, hoping that her babies would be left alone long enough for her to remove them at a later time and under the cover of darkness.

More often than not, these busy public officials arrived at the Ford Menagerie, toting a box of young, so-called abandoned critters. All of them in need of that little tender-loving-care. These district game wardens certainly didn't have the time to raise a family of young raccoons in addition to their busy twenty-four-hour duties. The wardens definitely had enough on their plates, just patrolling and answering the many complaints within their assigned districts.

After loudly voicing her negative thoughts as to why these wild animals had been so cruelly taken away from their dens, Mother quickly sprang into action by tending to that special care these animals so desperately needed. She'd inspect each of them very carefully, searching for injuries or any problems requiring special attention. Finding none, she'd then prepare a special dietary formula to start the feeding process.

It didn't take long before the little tykes adapted to the rubber teat on a baby's bottle. A bottle filled with a combination of warm pasteurized and evaporated milk. Occasionally, a small dose of Kaopectate was added into the mixture, in order to control the diarrhea that so often accompanied a new and unfamiliar diet. Thankfully it served its purpose quite well.

Nourishment and a regular diet were a big step in getting these critters started on a regular feeding schedule. In most cases their beady-eyes were yet to open, as they blindly latched their mouths around the rubber teat, aggressively sucking at the formula, while humming a tune of pleasure for the treat they were receiving. Those sounds of contentment during a feeding frenzy sounded like several small gasoline engines idling and purring away in a rhythm all their own. All of them were cranking in a well-orchestrated rhythm.

During lunch, they'd sprawl out on their backsides, gently cradled in our laps. Their little paws were constantly reaching and scratching for whatever they could touch, as they consumed as much of the warm milk as possible. Once they had enough to

8

eat, they were then placed in a warm bed made out of a cardboard box. The box was layered with soft towels as a lining. This box would become their den until such time when they could eat on their own and were allowed to roam wherever they cared to go. Inside of the box were a couple of quart bottles of hot tap water, wrapped in soft towels. These warm water bottles provided these critters with the warmth they'd have gotten had their mother been laying alongside of them.

After consuming a satisfying lunch, it didn't take long before they cuddled up close to one another, drifting off into a deep slumber. They'd sleep for hours on end, seldom making a peep.

A few hours later, when the desire for another meal came and when a little personal care was required, they were quick to let someone know it was that happy meal time again. Once one of them began crawling around inside the box indicating it was chow time, the entire litter would then start screaming bloody murder. There left little doubt that it once again was chow time!

Hearing them yowling as loud as they possibly could, you'd have thought they were starving, as evidenced from the commotion they made from all that scratching and climbing coming from inside the cardboard box. When it was feeding time, we dropped whatever we were doing in order to accommodate them. These feeding sessions really became a family affair. It required a lot of work and patience. With a sudden change in diets, the new milk formula occasionally caused a case of diarrhea for the little tykes.

Whenever diarrhea occurred with any of them, they managed to carry it throughout their tightly confined den, as they blindly crawled all over one another, spreading the runny and smelly feces throughout the entire box. It wasn't a pleasant scene by any sense of the imagination! When a case of diarrhea consumed the litter box, a thorough cleansing of the den and all of the kittens was required. One by one, a warm bath was given, rinsing away the feces that was coating them from one end to the other. It was during those times when I purposely made myself as scarce as possible! I didn't mind helping with the feeding sessions, but getting involved in a messy clean-up was something I wisely decided to let my mother handle. She was so much better at it than I was.

Upon receiving these small creatures from the authorities, she'd quickly determine their sex, while assigning an appropriate name to each one of them – names that would remain with them for the duration of their stay at the menagerie. I never really knew how her choice of names ever came about, but there were some good ones.

For instance, there was Little Willie, Big Willie, Tommy, Georgie, Katie, and a young male named Tater-Bug, plus several more I've since forgotten. Big Willie and Tater-Bug were my two favorites. Although Georgie was right up there on the list.

All of these little masked bandits would have been great subjects for a book relating to their own wild antics, had only we taken the time to document their many escapades. Especially one special hellion that she named Tater-Bug.

Tater-Bug was an extremely mischievous and inquisitive little critter. He was always seen scurrying about the countryside, living in what I considered to be a life similar to that of a cat. He appeared to have had nine lives, if not more, considering the many messes he often found himself in. But some of those catastrophes are stories for a little later.

A word to the wise – anyone desiring to share a similar lifestyle of raising wild animals on their own should be well aware of the fact that it involves a whole lot of dedicated time, a lot of hard work, a special type of patience, and care. It takes countless hours and a whole lot of personal dedication to reap the rewards of success. The end results weren't always what we hoped. But once we were committed to the process, there could be no quitting!

I considered myself very fortunate to have been living in amongst a wildlife menagerie. For a youngster such as I, it was a very special time in my life. Especially having the chance to meet the many wardens who were stopping by our home to drop off some wild critter or to check on how those creatures they'd left off earlier were doing. Often these warden visits were simply for a quick cup of coffee and a chance to share a little friendly conversation, but it was quite obvious they really cared about the many critters they'd delivered for rehab.

Those frequent warden visits, for a youngster like me, were a personal highlight. Listening to them relating their many adventures and witnessing how much they loved their careers, had me thinking that perhaps I would like to one day become a Maine Game Warden.

As I was starting my high school years, like most kids in my class, I was beginning to plan out what course of direction I wanted to take choosing my own future. I already knew what I most desired, and what I hoped my life's profession would become. I was intent on following that dream of one day becoming a State of Maine Game Warden. It was all I ever thought about. I was determined, come hell or high water, to follow in these wardens' footsteps if at all possible, no matter how long it took, or how hard I tried. Not until that last ray of hope had disappeared and the odds of ever being employed were completely gone, would I give up. I was determined!

Memorable Wild Guests at the Menagerie

My mother had certainly developed a lengthy list of rescued wild critters over the years. The undertaking of that wildlife care for the sake of saving the wild animals brought to our home was done at her own expense and on her own time.

Accepting the many tasks and challenges involved represented the sheer dedication and the great love of the wildlife that she possessed. My mother's rehabilitating activities and skills were accomplished with the full support of the warden service and the many area game wardens in southern Maine. But then again, it should have been. After all, they were the ones providing her with most of the wild critters she was trying to save.

As I look back upon those earlier years, Fritzi, the male fisher, was by far my favorite critter of them all. I was just starting high school when he arrived at our home. He was nothing more than a small bundle of cold and lifeless fur, obviously only a few days old when we received him. Fritzi was as near death as any animal we'd ever taken in. His eyes had yet to open. He was extremely cold and motionless.

In order to keep him alive Mother had to force feed the poor little tyke through an eye-dropper stuck through his lips, in hopes of getting him started onto a feeding ritual. His small and nearly lifeless body easily fit in the palm of a hand.

With that very first forced feeding, Fritzi started to come around. Although his movements were very slow and labored, he at least was eating what little he was being fed through the eye dropper.

In no time he became more active. We all took turns feeding him whenever meal time came around. Even then, Fritzi's survival was still quite questionable at best. But survive he did!

13

In no time, he quickly progressed and was rapidly growing into a handsome wildlife specimen. Fritzi and I bonded in what could be considered as a trusting relationship. A loving relationship of sorts that was quite similar to that of a young boy and his faithful dog. I'd wake up at night with Fritzi sleeping on my pillow or finding him sleeping at the foot of my bed. Having a fisher sleeping on your bed was quite an unusual experience for a young lad my age. Fritzi's story is a book in itself. A story that I'll share later on in this book.

My mother with Fritzi and one of the young raccoon
residents living at the menagerie

Always a New Critter Coming into the Menagerie

Those area game wardens in southern Maine certainly recognized my mother's dedication to the care of wild animals as evidenced by the many trips they made to our home.

They readily seized upon the opportunity to rid themselves from having to handle these young wild creatures in distress, knowing full well that these wild animals would receive the best care possible with my mother.

She was by no means an expert in the rehabilitating field. But she certainly had a keen sense and a God-given knowledge of how to properly care for those wild creatures she took in. There were no written demands and qualifications required for caring for wildlife during those times. Nothing like the many state restrictions required for those accepting wildlife care today.

Today's regulations all but demand for a person to be a registered, highly-trained veterinarian in order to have such a position. This is just another prime example of how the times have drastically changed over the years.

Rabies was seldom heard of during that era. The biggest medical crisis facing some of those wild critters coming into our home was an occasional case of distemper. Distemper being a virus that attacks the respiratory system of animals. Distemper is a very contagious disease and, as such, it required those animals suspected of having contracted it to either be put down or widely separated from the other animals.

Sadly, distemper claimed the life of a few of the animals dropped off at the menagerie. Each one of these losses was a great let-down for us personally, especially after having invested so much time and effort into their care.

Through it all, my mother treated every critter brought into our house as though she was their surrogate mother. She raised

15

them with the goal of hopefully returning them back into the wilderness where they truly belonged.

From early spring right through the summer months we received a variety of wild animals brought to us by the wardens patrolling their southern Maine districts.

The Wardens

Many of the game wardens patrolling the Southern Maine region had become great family friends in those earlier days. The list included: District Wardens Verne Walker, Charlie Libby, George Townsend, and Supervisors Maynard Marsh, Charlie Allen, Mickey Noble, and Donis Wheaton, along with District Wardens Don Gray, Russ Dyer, John Marsh, and a few others who occasionally came through our doors.

I always anticipated their many visits, while intently listening to their many stories and adventures. No one rendition was ever the same. These wardens and the enjoyable lifestyles they were living became the inspiration for one day to be following in their footsteps.

The pursuit of that dream certainly was helped along by Warden Pilot George Townsend, at a time when I was a student in grammar school. George often flew down from Rangeley where he lived, in order to fly the district wardens in southern Maine.

A few days prior to his arrival he'd have a barrel of aviation fuel dropped off at our house. Once he arrived in the area, he would tether the plane on the ice behind our home overnight. George would stay with us during that short period of time he was in the area. As a youngster, I anxiously anticipated seeing that small yellow and red piper cub, circling low over the house upon his arrival.

One day my brother, Gerald, and I were skating on the pond when George brought the plane in for a landing. I'll never forget his motioning for us to come over to the small airplane, "How would you boys like to go up for a little flight?" he inquired. What kid in his right mind would ever refuse the experience of a flight with one of Maine's finest? That memory of my first airplane ride would always be a highlight in my young life.

Unfortunately, a few years later, George's name was added to the Fallen Officers Memorial in Augusta as one of the game wardens killed in the line of duty.

George and an area biologist were both killed on Maranacook Lake in the town of Readfield when the new department plane George was piloting crashed during take-off. The seat pin holding the pilot's seat somehow slipped out during the takeoff, forcing George to unexpectedly slide backwards. This sudden action caused the plane to flip over in the air and fall from the sky. They hit the water, wings first, and as a result they both drowned.

George Townsend in my book was a hero, and certainly a person whom I idolized as an inspiration to my wanting to follow along in his footsteps.

As time moved on, that dream of one day becoming a game warden myself was all I ever could think about. Come hell or high water, I intended to pursue that profession. I vowed to never give up the pursuit until the last straw had been cast and all hopes of ever fulfilling the dream had been diminished. I wanted to dedicate my life to the out-of-doors, just like they were doing.

Living the dream and serving the public just as these men were doing was my main goal in life. But for now, I had a long way to go. I was still in high school, seeking that signed diploma that I'd need in order to keep the dream alive.

In addition to the many wild animals coming through our doors, there were several owls, hawks, partridges, ducks, and a wide variety of songbirds that, for one reason or another, ventured into the menagerie over the years.

We never knew what kind of wild creature we'd be helping Mom with next. They all had their own separate distinct personalities. Each of them being a story in itself.

As I look back in the diaries, I recall Dolly, a fawn that was only a few days old when we inherited her. She was cute as a button!

There was Dolly, a fawn that was as cute as a button!

And then there was Bucky, a small buck deer recovering from a leg injury. He became the king of our back yard, assuming security duty around the premises, while protecting the property against intruders that he didn't know, from entering our barn. The barn was his place to stay at night or whenever the weather outside was miserable. Bucky would only allow those he recognized to enter through its doors. All the others did so at their own risk!

In addition to the many memorable furry critters hanging out in the den, there was Hooty, a mature Great Horned Owl that stayed with us for a few months. Hooty had the free rein inside our house from just before Christmas of 1963 until February of the following year. Hooty was nurtured back to good health after apparently consuming a dose of rat poison at a local dump.

Gerald, my brother, found both Hooty and an Arctic Snowy Owl laying on the ground at the Berwick dump. Both of these owls were near death as he scooped them up, bringing them to the menagerie where hopefully they might get another chance of living a normal life.

Apparently, some type of a rodent poison had been placed around the grounds of the outdoor dump in an effort to cut down on the large number of rats living in amongst the open garbage. Town dumps in those days were known for hosting a large quantity of rodents in their landfills.

Both owls were weak and near death when my brother brought them home. A quick den was made out of a couple of large cardboard boxes, with raw hamburger and water left at their disposal. These ingredients were hopefully either going to save them or not.

From the appearances of watching these owls, once we shut the lights off that evening, it was doubtful they'd survive the night. There was very little, if any, signs of life shown in either of them. Sadly, the Snowy Owl didn't make it through the night. But upon checking the box early the next morning, looking for the Great Horned Owl, he wasn't to be found.

We quickly searched every room in the house looking for Hooty, wondering where in the blazes he could have gone. Finally, I spotted two big yellow eyes and a feathered head bobbing up and down, peering out from the bottom branches of our Christmas tree that was strategically located in the bay windows of our living room. Hooty was cautiously watching our every move. It was quite a sight to behold! How many folks do you suppose ever had a Great Horned Owl decorating their Christmas tree?

Hooty stayed from December through late February. Every day saw a marked improvement in his health. Hooty actually was quite tame, all things considered. He allowed us to gently touch and feed him. He'd snap his beak together like a pair of scissors rapidly being open and closed, indicating his displeasure in having us encroaching upon his space, but it was all for show. Never once did the owl attack or attempt to strike at us with those razor-sharp talons it possessed. Talons that could raise holy old havoc if they struck where they were intended.

Hooty made it through the night and went on to reach eventual freedom

Finally, in mid-February, when the owl started hooting in the middle of the night while flying from room to room, we decided it was time to send him on his way. After all, it was mating season for the owls and this one was definitely on the prowl. There's nothing more annoying than trying to sleep when you have an "owl on the prowl," inside the house.

Once back outside, Hooty quickly took to the skies in what hopefully was a long life ahead. I did have to admit though, it was kind of unique waking up in the middle of the night, listening to the loud sounds of an owl hooting in the next room from where you were sleeping. This was what experiencing life at the menagerie was like. We always were expecting the unexpected. That was the norm around our house. Especially with so many wild critters roaming freely throughout the menagerie. All of them creating their own share of priceless memories. Memories that I'll never forget.

A Raccoon Named Tater-Bug

Tater-Bug was by far the most memorable of all the raccoons coming through the menagerie. His unpredictable actions always kept us on our toes.

It was in the spring of 1963 when Game Warden Charlie Libby arrived at our house toting a small shoe box containing a young male raccoon.

Tater-Bug – a raccoon with nine lives

Warden Libby's district covered the coastal area of Wells, Maine. There were several summer camps located within his patrol area. Many of these camps and outbuildings provided a fair share of the wild creatures brought to our sanctuary for that tender-loving-care my mother provided.

This particular baby raccoon was found abandoned in an elderly lady's shed. Apparently, its mother had been moving her kittens to a safer location after being scared away from the residence by the owners. In her haste of relocating them, she'd apparently left one behind. The small bundle of fur was lying motionless inside the small box that Charlie was holding.

"I don't know if this one's going to make it, Butch. He seems to be in pretty tough shape," Charlie stated. "We left him lying there by the outside shed for a few more hours, hoping that maybe the mother might return. But she never did!" he claimed.

"Butch," was a nickname given to my mother by her father. My mother was considered to be the "Tom Boy" of the family at an early age, and without a doubt she was! She'd much rather have been outside hunting or fishing, or dealing with some wild critter, than to be playing with dolls and doing those "girly things" that the girls her age were so noted for.

My mother could kill and dress off a deer, dragging it out of the woods by herself, just as well, if not better, than any man! She didn't hesitate chopping her own firewood and starting the fires, keeping the ice fishing shack warm, while she fished for freshwater smelts on Mousam Lake in the bitter cold of winter.

Lots of times because of the deep snow she had to park her vehicle far away from the pond. By donning a pair of snowshoes she'd hike down through the deep snow the mile or so to the lake, where the small smelt fishing shanty village was located out on the pond. Once there, she snagged more of those little silvery fish than anyone else around her, to the amazement of those who weren't catching any.

Freshwater smelt fishing was accomplished with a hand line and a small hook, baited with pieces of cut bait. Smelting was a family pastime for our entire family during the cold winter months. It was a pastime that we thoroughly enjoyed. The comradeship established with the other fishermen was priceless. So it was, that my mother had inherited the nickname, "Butch."

As usual, she was extremely concerned about this newest addition to the menagerie as she reached into the box, carefully scooping up the small bundle of fur up into her hands. It was obvious this little fellow was in rough shape. He was barely moving and seemed to be extremely cold and lifeless.

However, as she slowly ran her finger across his mouth, he quickly latched onto it with a sucking sound, obviously thinking it was a teat and that his dinner was about to be served.

"If we can get a little milk into him Charlie, I think he'll be fine," she enthusiastically said. Placing the little tyke back into the box, she quickly hurried out into the kitchen whipping up a batch of that special formula she used just for such occasions – the same formula that had sustained so many of the other small critters left in her care.

In no time the little fellow was straddled in her lap, furiously consuming the warm milk that hopefully would keep him alive. His little paws were reaching skyward and flailing wildly, almost as if he was reaching for the heavens. All the while he was loudly purring in obvious pleasure, while feverishly drinking the milk from the baby bottle.

"Look at him go! He was just about starved to death!" she stated. "He reminds me of a little bug, with those little paws and feet furiously grasping for anything nearby," she sputtered. "I think that's a good name for him. I think we'll call this one "Tater-Bug," she declared.

And thus Tater-Bug became the newest addition to the Ford Menagerie. And a wild one he was! Tater-Bug despised being left alone in his little den of tangled towels and hot water bottles. He'd yowl and carry on seeking a little special attention and affection. Especially at feeding time. None of the critters before him had been anywhere near as vocal. But then again, none of the others were left all alone and confined in a cardboard box!

Tater-Bug knew if he screeched loud enough, eventually he'd get that attention he was seeking. He loved being held and played with. He simply couldn't get enough of it!

The Bug had yet to open his eyes. But even with his eyes closed, he somehow managed to find a means of escaping the cardboard den, finding his way to one of us, seeking that attention he so desperately desired. Perhaps that's why he was abandoned in the first place. Maybe he'd crawled too far away from the den for his mother to find him.

Tater-Bug had an independent personality and a distinct means of getting into more trouble than all of the young raccoons before him combined. During the summer months, Tater-Bug grew from a small ball of fur into a handsome young raccoon. He was allowed to come and go from the house as he pleased. The food bucket was always full, and his old den was readily available should he decide to return home.

Tater-Bug was living what one might consider as the "life-of-Riley!" It was nothing for the Bug to be gone for days on end, only eventually ending up a few miles away in some compromising situation where he had to be rescued by the matriarch of our family. The entire neighborhood wasn't surprised if the Bug suddenly arrived scratching on their door. They'd simply give us a call and we'd come to his aid. The Bug was definitely a wanderer.

But whenever he suddenly re-appeared, it seemed as though it wasn't without some catastrophic event taking place. Such as the time he ended up in a complete stranger's dooryard, better than a half mile from home, with a can firmly stuck on his head. The neighbor, realizing that probably it was our Tater Bug, called for yet another rescue. Sure enough, there he was. Tater-Bug was blindly bumping and staggering into things like a drunken sailor who'd been on a big bender after riding the waves for several months on end. It was hard to determine just how long he'd been entangled with the can stuck to his head. But judging from the looks of his scrawny body, he'd been "in-the-can" for a while.

Once again, Tater-Bug ended up at a place where his rescue was made possible. Upon hearing my mother's calming voice, he immediately headed toward her for yet another save. Tater-Bug was certainly using up his chances of survival. What were the chances that he'd emerge from the woods or wherever he had been, ending up in a place where a rescue would save him, yet again. He definitely was like a cat with nine lives.

However, the most memorable rescue of the Bug came from the Sanford Police Department on Sunday evening, February 9, 1964. That evening was a time in musical history that some of you older folks might remember. By older, I mean people my age!

A brutal winter storm was hitting our area, with blinding snow and howling winds. The driving was treacherous, if not damn near impossible. "Tater bug," had been amongst the missing for a few weeks. But like so many of the raccoons before him, we simply assumed he'd reverted back into the wilderness and was gone for good. Although to have done so in the middle of winter was a rarity.

On that particular evening our family was anxiously gathered around the small black and white television set that provided us with several hours of entertainment. Just having a television set in those days was quite a treat. On this evening history was about to change in the musical world. The days and sounds of Sinatra and Presley were being challenged by a long-haired group of four British foreigners, "The Fab 4," or the so-called "Beatles."

We were anxiously awaiting the Ed Sullivan show to begin, as the Beatles were about to make their American debut, when suddenly the phone rang. It was the Sanford Police Department, inquiring if we were the folks who cared for wild animals.

"We are!" my mother said, wondering what kind of a critter they'd possibly rescued under these wintery conditions.

"Sorry to bother you ma'am," the dispatcher said, "but a local Springvale resident was just alarmed by a scratching at their door. Assuming that it was blowing snow that needed immediate removal, they opened the door, only to have a small raccoon come bounding into their kitchen just as if he lived there," the dispatcher chuckled. "The complainant said the raccoon stood up on his hind feet, balancing himself as if he was looking for a handout of grub. Fortunately, these folks determined this raccoon had to have been someone's pet. Instead of panicking and disposing of the little twerp, they've locked him in a closet," the dispatcher snickered. "One of our officers suggested we give you a call to see if this might be one of yours," he quipped.

And so it was. On a blustery and cold February night, my folks struck out on yet another Tater-Bug rescue mission, in a blinding snowstorm, to bring the Bug back home again. This time he was more than six miles away from home.

Like so many times before, the Bug amazingly ended up in a place where his rescue was once again made possible. He was quite happy to see his adopted mother coming through the door, as he quickly ran to her side and climbed up into her arms.

Eventually Tater Bug left the menagerie and never returned. Like all the other guests who had lived and roamed at the menagerie, it was only a matter of time before he too would simply disappear, leaving behind a whole lot of pleasant memories. Memories that were priceless.

Preparing for the Future

After finally graduating from high school, my main goal in life was still to hopefully secure a position as a Maine Game Warden. Seeking a warden's position with the fish and game department was all I ever thought about.

Back home the living arrangements had drastically changed within our family shortly after I had completed my school years. Like so many other families, my parents had amicably divorced and they each had gone their separate ways. My mother continued on with her work, caring for wild animals.

In the meantime, she had remarried the local game warden, Verne Walker. The marriage came as no big surprise. It was obvious they had many of the same interests and had been involved in a secret courtship that had been ongoing for quite some time.

The amicable parting of the ways by my parents really came as no surprise to anyone. I offered my support and love to both of them, knowing full well that for a long time things had not really been copacetic between them. My dad was strong and charismatic and I knew in time his life would be happier. I was sure he'd be the stronger by starting over in a new life. I also knew he'd support my efforts in whatever profession I chose to pursue, including that as a Maine Game Warden.

By then I was pretty well off on my own. I had joined the United States Air Force in 1966, one year after graduating from high school. I was hoping to see the world at the government's expense before returning to Maine in pursuit of that warden's career I so desperately wanted. The requirements of a warden's job in the late 1960s were extremely minimal compared to those of today. A candidate back in those days had to be 21 years of age. They had to have a signed high school diploma, had to be 5 feet 8 inches tall, weigh at least 158 pounds and must have passed a written exam along with a thorough background investigation by the department as to their demeanor and credibility. That basically was it!

Upon meeting those requirements, a candidate's name was then placed on an eligibility list while waiting for openings to occur, either from retirements or from an illness of one of the agency's members. The warden's career in those days was quite competitive. It was a highly sought-after profession by many young men seeking a new career – men like myself, all of them hoping to experience a profession of living in the out-of-doors, dealing with the wildlife and the sportsmen of our state. Like myself, all of these candidates were looking to *"Live the Dream!"*

Notice that I referred to the male gender only. During this time, only the qualified males were considered for employment as game wardens. The sexual discrimination laws of today were completely unheard of at that time. Females simply were not considered for a law enforcement position.

It wasn't until 1978, when Deborah Palman joined the agency as the first female game warden to have been assigned to her own district. The times were rapidly changing. Remarkably, Debbie showed the world that the warden's job wasn't designed strictly for males only. She was as capable of performing her duties as her counterparts, if not more than some.

Today the warden force consists of several female officers. All of them are enjoying the same traditions that we males previously had held to ourselves. What once had been a totally male profession changed in 1978.

In July of 1966, I voluntarily signed up with the United States Air Force right during the controversial Vietnam War, much to the disgruntlement of my family. I was eager to travel and see the big world at the government's expense before seriously pursuing that game warden's dream I so badly wanted. What better way to see the world before coming back to Maine to eventually settle down in hopefully what would become a great career. And what better way to see this big world of ours than to do it at the government's expense!

This sudden and rather dramatic life-changing event actually turned out to be God's way of putting me in the right place at the right time. If ever there was such a thing as divine intervention, it was happening right before my eyes.

I was sent to Lackland AFB in Texas for the usual basic military training and then on to Biloxi, Mississippi, for technical training as a radar operator. While at Biloxi, the instructor inquired if it were possible for any of us trainees to go anywhere in the world, what two places would we like to go upon completion of our training?

I boldly stated that my first choice would be a trip to Vietnam. A place where, thanks to the draft, many of my classmates had been sent right out of school. I fully expected to do my patriotic chore when I joined the military, while at the same time I was hoping to get to see a part of the world that I never knew existed.

My second choice was to be sent to Alaska, I wisely stated. The instructor, chuckling in total hysteria said, "Alaska! Alaska! Why in hell do you want to go to Alaska? No one ever asks to go to Alaska!" he comically sputtered.

Proudly, I explained my goal in life was to one day become a Maine Game Warden. "What better place to go than where there's great fishing and lots of wildlife, than in the great state of Alaska!" I smartly replied.

He quickly responded, "Well son, if I were you, I wouldn't be getting your heavy Air Force parka out, because where you'll be going, you won't be needing it!" he snickered. Hinting that more than likely, Vietnam would definitely become my next assignment.

Meanwhile back home, my parents were having a fit. They were petrified that I was about to be sent into the war zone in southeast Asia, like so many of my classmates before me.

31

Sadly some of those classmates were returning home in body bags, casualties of the controversial war. Upon the arrival of my assignment orders, I called home to a mother who obviously was a nervous wreck. I could sense the pent-up emotions and the fear in her voice when she rather hesitantly asked, "So where are you going to be going?"

I knew that she had assumed I'd be headed far away, right into the war zone. I stated, "You aren't going to believe this Ma, but do you have a Maine map handy?"

There was a slight pause before she asked, "Why do I need that?" I could tell that she was about ready to have a nervous breakdown when I responded, "Strange as it is, my orders are for a small air force base located in some place called Topsham, Maine. I don't have a clue where Topsham is, do you?" I calmly inquired.

Go figure! I was being sent back to Maine, during a time of war, assigned to a small air base that was located less than sixty miles from home. So much for seeing the world at the government's expense. I was home more than I was in the service.

Remarkably however, I believe that particular assignment was God's way of putting me in the right place at the right time. Especially when during my third year of being stationed at the small radar base, I was allowed to take the written game warden's exam in Augusta.

Augusta was located a mere thirty miles from the base and the base commander obligingly allowed me the opportunity to take the test! But then again, he should have. You see he was a Canadian Colonel, and upon my arrival at the base I immediately was called into his office.

Afraid I was going to be sent elsewhere and being quite leery of that high-ranking chain of command, I really didn't know what to expect. Reporting to the Colonel as ordered and having that strict military structure of command that had just been drilled into my head for the past several weeks, he immediately put me at ease.

The gist of the meeting was totally unexpected. He heard I was from Maine and knowing that the hunting season was about to start, his inquiry was a rather personal inquiry, whether I hunted or not? I told him that I did.

Do you know of any place where maybe you could take a few of us officers deer hunting? he asked.

I certainly did, my mother and stepfather, Verne Walker, had purchased a large parcel of land in the town of Shapleigh, less than 60 miles away from the air base known as the Vernon Walker Game Management Area.

My first official assignment was to take the Colonel and a few officers hunting in an area that today is known as the Vernon Walker Game Management Area, located in North Shapleigh. This military career wasn't so bad after all, I thought!

As a side note, three of the officers came back with deer. It had been a very successful day and I now had some important military friends for life. So when I asked for the time to take the most important test in my life, the colonel was quite happy to oblige.

I did report to Augusta, where miraculously I passed both exams, including the background check, with no other issues holding me back from possibly fulfilling that dream I envisioned. My name was then placed on an eligibility list for consideration for future employment, should an opening occur and if I was readily available.

By the Grace of God and a whole lot of good fortune, I was one step closer to actually realizing that warden dream I was harboring. None of this would have been possible, had the military sent me elsewhere in the big world. To this very day, I honestly consider my original assignment at the Topsham Airbase to be an act of divine intervention. That same divine intervention which has followed and sheltered my life's journey on more than one occasion.

Finally, I now had an inside connection with the fish and game department, minor as it might have been. The only drawback being my immediate availability for fish and game, as I still had a full year to go to finish my military obligation with Uncle Sam. The eligibility list, as I understood it, would be held for three years or more. I only hoped that I'd eventually have the chance to be drawn from that list and to be selected to present my case in the hiring process.

Shortly after making the warden eligibility list, the military designated the small Topsham airbase for closure. The radar unit that was the main purpose of operation at the small air base, was now obsolete. So the government decided to shut the entire outfit down and to close the base.

I just might get to see the big old world after all, seeing that I still had one more year of military obligation to go. But instead of traveling across the world as I had hoped, I was sent a few miles north to yet another small air base located in Charleston, Maine. So much for hoping to see the big world, especially on the government's dime! And to think I had purposely joined the military during a time of war, hoping to travel the big globe at the government's expense, only to spend all but a few weeks of my military career less than a hundred and fifty miles from home. Go figure!

But by now, I honestly didn't care where they sent me. All I cared about was being available for that warden's career if and when that time ever came. For now, it seemed as though all time was at a complete standstill. I didn't think the day would ever come when I no longer was tied to Uncle Sam's coat tails, knowing that the life's dream I had envisioned was lingering off in the future. But the day finally arrived when my military obligations had been fulfilled and I was, in the words of Martin Luther King, "Free at last! Free at last!"

On July 20, 1970, I departed the Charleston radar base for the very last time, headed to Sanford in pursuit of a job and yet another means of financial existence. At the age of 23, I was now eligible for employment with the Fish and Game Department, if an opportunity for employment ever arose and if that eligibility list from a few years earlier was still active. I quickly secured a job as a handyman with W.T. Grant, a small department store located in South Sanford. The pay was minimal and the job certainly was not the future I was looking forward to. But at least having a steady source of income and keeping busy was better than nothing at all. I was still dreaming about securing that warden career, but by now a lot of time had passed by. I wasn't even sure if the eligibility list that I'd been counting on was still active. For the first time, I was beginning to wonder if I'd ever get to live that dream after all.

I moved back in with my mother and the local game warden, Verne Walker. Verne was like a family member long before my parents' divorce ever came about. I felt bad for the family I knew as a kid changing, but for their sake I was very happy for the both of them. I seized every opportunity I possibly could to go on patrol with Verne. Just witnessing the professional approach Verne used during his many contacts with the public was extremely impressive to say the least. Even when he was communicating with some of those he'd held accountable for past violations, they all seemed quite pleased to be around him. Having witnessed that experience of patrolling and observing a real pro in action taught me so much. Verne knew how badly I wanted to be one of the gang, as he kept offering his words of encouragement. "Have patience, your time will come if it is meant to be," he advised. Having that wisdom and support from a veteran warden was priceless.

On the other hand, as the time was quickly passing by, I was beginning to think the dream was exactly that, nothing more than a fantasy and a wishful thought! That all changed early one September morning, when Verne came rushing into the department store. Rather excitedly he said, "I hear you're going to be called to Augusta for an interview regarding a couple of game warden positions that the department has coming up," he rather excitedly spouted. If I didn't know better, I think he was as excited, if not more so, than I was! And I have to say, I was some damn excited. Verne cautiously explained, "Not to discourage you John, but don't plan on getting hired the very first time around. More than likely, they'll want to see just how serious you are about pursuing the job," he warned. "They'll be watching you closely," he advised. "Should you get rejected the first time around and you still persist on returning for future interviews, then they'll know that you are seriously seeking a warden's job," he calmly stated. "Go for that interview, seeing it as yet another opportunity and another great chance to get your foot in the door," he said. "It will be a good opportunity for you to meet those in charge, and a chance to get acquainted with those who will remember you in the future," he wisely stated.

Verne's words were somewhat discouraging, but his well-meant advice made perfect sense, especially realizing just how competitive these jobs had become. If I needed to go to Augusta more than once to secure the dream, I definitely planned on going as many times as it would take, or until they politely advised me never to bother coming back again!

The very next day I received the official notice of the upcoming interview in the mail. I was directed to report to the Deputy Chief Warden, Jack Shaw, at 09:30 a.m. on September 8th, 1970, for an employment interview. Once again I felt the adrenaline rushing into my veins and a flow of that same sense of excitement, just thinking about the possibility of securing a warden's position that had been constantly on my mind, 24 hours a day.

And now suddenly I was one step closer to living the dream.

The Interview and a Dream Come True

Deputy Chief Warden William J. Shaw

I headed for Augusta early on the morning of September 8th, 1970. The interview was scheduled for 9:30, but I was on the road nervously heading that way at the very first sign of daybreak. I don't think I slept a wink the night before, as I anxiously anticipated what to expect during this interview. Verne and my mother offered a wide variety of suggestions as to how I should act and what types of questions I might be asked during the process. I think they were as nervous, if not more so, than what I was. God had been with me every inch of the way so far. I simply prayed that he'd be there once again today!

Arriving in Augusta, way earlier than my scheduled appointment, I rode the elevator up to the sixth floor of the State office building where the Fish and Game Department was located. I patiently sat outside the office, watching as other people were coming and going from their own interviews. The secretary eventually escorted me into a hallway, where I was greeted by Deputy Chief Warden, William "Jack" Shaw. Jack quickly ushered me into his rather small and cramped office. His stern appearance and larger-than-life frame certainly were a bit intimidating. He appeared to be very serious and obviously was all business, as he sat down behind his plush desk facing my way. Not knowing what to expect, I nervously seated myself in front of him. I couldn't help noticing that he seemed to be visually scanning and checking me all over. He appeared to be looking me up and down as if he was doing some sort of a human body scan, like a TSA agent at one of our airports. And he was doing it without so much as uttering a word. Finally after what seemed like forever, he cleared his throat and, with a big smile and a slight nod of his head, he looked at me as he winked and inquired, "Are you by any chance single?" Honestly speaking, the unexpected question scared the living hell out of me. Maybe it was a case of paranoia or just plain nerves, but the unexpected question seemed to be quite personal and was asked in a rather seductive way! I began secretly scanning the room for the exit signs, should I feel the need to make a sudden escape! I nervously replied, "Yes sir, I am!" All the while I was wondering what the heck he is going to ask me next. My fears were quickly calmed, when he stated, "That's good, we are looking for a young single man for a district we have open," he calmly stated. "Someone who is single and looking to make a career in a district that we currently have an immediate opening for!" he quickly explained. "Actually there are two districts available. One is a remote Maine town known as Daaquam. Daaquam is only accessible by going into Canada and coming back down a tote road adjacent to the Maine/N.H. and the Canadian border," he stated. "Very few folks live there at any given time," he quietly mumbled. "Now I doubt a young single fellow like yourself, looking to start a new career, would ever enjoy the solitude of a place like Daaquam," he bluntly sputtered. "First of all, you'd probably be woods queer inside of a week or two, and more importantly, you'd be hard pressed to find yourself a woman!" he chirped. "But the other district we have, is located in the northern section of Waldo County. The Burnham District!" he emphasized, as he pointed to a large State of Maine wall map hanging in back of him. "This district has some of the best deer hunting territory in our state," he stated. "But it's also noted for its ruthless and rampant poaching activity," he quickly added. "I want to be perfectly honest with you, John. There are a few folks up there who hate game wardens," he disgustedly sputtered. "To prove their point, recently late at night while the district warden was off working, these thugs shot out and threw rocks through nearly every window of our state-owned camp, while the warden's wife and young daughter lay huddled together on the floor, thinking they were about to die," he disgustedly stated. "Those poor people were terrified by the sounds of the breaking window glass, coupled with the shotgun blasts into the air and having the rocks landing all around them," he stated. "Unfortunately, it took the warden and the state police a long while to get there," Jack rather angrily quipped. "Needless to say, this warden and his family no longer wish to live there," he rather somberly stated.

It was quite obvious from the expression on Jack's face, he was emotionally distraught by this inexcusable act of violence directed toward a member of his warden's family. "We've put this district out to bid to the other 119 wardens in the state, looking for someone who wants to transfer down to that area. But not a one of them seems to be interested," he solemnly explained. "So, we're looking for a single man, John. Someone who is willing to start a new career in an area where they might never be welcomed. By any chance is that someone you?" he bluntly inquired.

Without hesitating, I boldly stated, "Sir, I'll go anywhere in the state of Maine where you'd want me to go." What appeared to be a rather mild sense of relief, Jack stated, "Good, John! When can you start?" he inquired. I wasn't sure if I'd heard him right, when anxiously I asked, "Does that mean I've got the job?"

"Well damn it, you do want it don't you?" he kind of disgustedly barked. Apparently in his line of thinking he thought I was back tracking!

"Oh yes sir, you don't know how badly I want it!" I quickly exclaimed. I'll never forget that precious moment. All those years of preparing and dreaming about becoming a game warden and suddenly here I am, officially being offered the job from the man in charge of the hiring. There were no words in existence that could describe the euphoric flood of pleasantries that were rushing into my head. Why you'd have thought I'd just won the Powerball Lottery and that all there was left to do was to claim the top prize! And what a prize it would be!

Jack grinning ever so slightly said, "Why don't you plan on returning here on September 22, after notifying your employer that you'll be leaving their employment," he stated. "You'll be sworn in at that time, making your position official," he advised. "Then you'll need to go to Federal Street where you'll get your uniforms and the equipment necessary to perform your new duties," he quipped.

With that being said, Jack stood up and with a strong and firm handshake, he welcomed me into the agency as its newest district game warden. A dozen sticks of dynamite couldn't have removed that excrement-eating grin from my face! Finally, after all these years, the dream came true! I hoped to be just like those great wardens I'd observed and got to know over the years. Experienced wardens like: Verne Walker, George Townsend, Charlie Libby, Maynard Marsh, Charlie Allen, Mickey Noble, Donis Wheaton, Vernon Moulton, Don Gray, Russ Dyer, Teddy Hanson, and John Marsh, just to name a few. Observing those professionals coming to our house, while delivering some wild critter or hanging around just for a quick cup of coffee and conversation, continuously ignited that burning desire of my wanting to become one of them. I looked upon the game warden's career not so much as a job, but more of a way of life.

Waiting to be officially sworn in as Maine's newest game warden was unbearable. Verne and my mother were ecstatic that I'd finally reached that long-awaited milestone in my life. One that I'd only dreamed about for years on end. I could tell they were extremely proud to say the least. Verne was totally surprised that I'd been hired so quickly and especially on the very first try. But later as time passed by, he kind of admitted how he felt the agency was in kind of a bind, considering the violence from that area and that the agency wanted to fill it as soon as possible, especially with the upcoming hunting season coming right up. "They needed to have a warden representative in that area, all things considered," he theorized. Whatever the situation might have been, I was one happy camper!

Taking the Oath – Living the Dream!

Upon my return from Augusta, I quickly notified the bosses at the department store that I'd soon be moving on. They were extremely supportive of the career change. During the interim, I ventured north where I connected with Warden Lowell Thomas, his wife Shirley, and their young daughter, Marsha. It was Lowell's district that I'd soon be inheriting. Listening to Shirley recall the frightening events of that fateful night, was like recounting a scene out of the wild, wild west. Back in those old western days when a sense of western anarchy prevailed. Just hearing about such a ruthless behavior in these modern times was rare.

Lowell suggested I tag along with him on patrol if I cared to go. It was a golden opportunity that I simply couldn't pass up! We patrolled the many towns and areas that I'd soon be responsible for. Lowell pointed out places of interest or a place where a suspected poacher was currently living. He introduced me to many of the citizens he thought I should become acquainted with. People who'd be willing to help me in a time of need. From the many stops we made, it was obvious that Lowell had earned the utmost respect from the majority of the citizens he represented. Sadly, it was a small gang of organized poachers who placed his family in jeopardy. A small gang of ruthless thugs that ended up driving them away. For the sake of his family, no one could certainly blame him.

Spending the day patrolling with Warden Lowell Thomas was priceless. I returned back home late that evening, all the more anxious for that moment in time when I'd be patrolling the region myself. September 22, 1970, couldn't come quick enough.

The Moment I Began Living the Dream

September 22, 1970, finally arrived. I barely slept the night before, anticipating the morning swearing-in ceremony. This day was going to be the biggest day in my life, bar none. The day when I'd actually start *"living the dream!"* I only hoped it wouldn't end up being a nightmare and that my expectations may have been more than what I had envisioned.

My folks had me up bright and early, providing a breakfast that was fit for a king. They were still somewhat amazed that I'd been hired so quickly, as Verne was offering a constant barrage of good sound advice. Advice as to what I should and should not do, once I got into my assigned area. Welcomed advice for sure!

"Just remember John, those people don't dislike you personally. It's the badge that you wear and the profession you've chosen that they disagree with," he quipped. "You're a threat to their illegal business," he cautioned. "If you treat them fairly and honestly, eventually you'll get their support and a sense of respect back. You've got to prove yourself to them," he said. "Don't approach them with a big chip on your shoulder, acting as though you're a bit better than they are," he warned. "If you do, I'll guarantee you that someone will knock that chip off and you'll hate every minute of your career from that point on," he seriously advised. "Whatever you do, don't take their actions personally. These guys are going to try to out-smart you day in and day out. And most of the time they're going to be successful. Just remember, it's a long road with no turns in it. If they are frequent poachers, you'll eventually get a crack at holding them accountable," he wisely stated.

This welcomed advice to a rookie just starting out in a law enforcement career without any experience, was again, priceless. Other than what I'd learned by listening, observing, and riding with a couple of the old pros, such as Warden Verne Walker and Warden Don Gray, admittedly I was as green as they come. These men both certainly inspired me into following the dream. The time I got to spend with them was a real learning experience.

After breakfast, I grabbed a few items before heading off to Augusta. I didn't have any idea as to when I might get back home again! During the long ride north, I wondered if I'd fit the mold of those wardens I had come to idolize. "Would I be accepted by the people I'd serve?" I silently thought, as I drove along the highway headed north. "Would I meet the expectations of the bosses who I knew would be watching me very closely?" I thought. "Even more so, would the wardens I'd be working with be as friendly and helpful as I'd hoped?" I pondered. After all, it had been the vicious actions of a few radicals within the district I'd soon be patrolling, that were the reason I'd been hired in the first place! "Eventually would these same thugs decide to challenge and try me too?" I wondered.

It was quite obvious that there were a few folks in the area who had absolutely no use for game wardens in general. With so many thoughts racing through my mind as I headed north, in no time at all I had arrived at the Fish and Game headquarters. This time I was cordially greeted by the Deputy Chief Warden, William Shaw, and Commissioners George Bucknam and Maynard Marsh. With little fanfare, Deputy Commissioner Marsh conducted the swearing-in ceremony making my position official. The secretary then presented several documents and papers that needed to be signed in order to complete the deal. Everything from health insurance forms to retirement papers were handed my way, one right after another. "Just sign here," I was told, as yet another bunch of papers were slid my way! Officially being sworn in as the newest member of the department, within a few hours I'd be turned loose upon the very public I'd be serving. The work ethics in those days were simply on-the-job training. A kind of learn-as-you-go attitude. Before the day's end, I'd basically be patrolling out on my own. In those days there was no advanced schooling, no training, no months of instruction as to how to perform the duties that I was expected to handle. I was informed that at some time in the future, I'd be going to a 12-week basic warden school that was to be held at the University of Maine in Orono.

In the meantime, I was out on my own. This certainly was a far cry from the employment procedures expected of today's officers. Today's candidates endure several weeks and even months of rigorous police academy training before being turned loose onto a wary public. I sometimes wonder if perhaps those strict requirements for today's warden curriculum might have come about due to the actions of those of us who simply tackled the in's and out's of the career as best we could by working on our own agenda!

After completing the huge bundle of paperwork making my position official, I was sent over to the Federal Street storehouse to acquire the equipment needed to perform my duties. Before leaving the main office, Jack stated, "Your radio call number will be 807. They'll explain the radio codes to you over at the storehouse," he quickly explained. "Also, you'll need to make a quick stop in Waterville on your way north for a physical confirming that you're healthy enough to assume your new duties. They'll be expecting you," he stated. "Finally, once you arrive in Burnham you'll meet up with Supervisor Charles Allen and Inspector Lee Downs at the Burnham warden's camp," he directed. "Welcome aboard and take care of yourself out there, John," Jack warmly stated, before sending me on my way. That long anticipated journey of *"Living the Dream"* was about to begin!

I Felt Like a Winner on a TV Game Show

At the storehouse I met, Wendell "Tiger" Symes, the agency's supply officer. Tiger was given the nickname because of his brashness in issuing the equipment to the men out in the field. "You'd think Tiger had to pay for this equipment out of his own pocket," it was said. But I found him to be more than gracious in providing my needs.

Wendell produced several uniforms, demanding that I try them on for a proper fit. The fall uniform consisted of blue wool pants and cotton shirts. As I stood before the mirror, I couldn't help but noticing the big grin on my face. I kept pinching myself to see if this was really happening or, if maybe, it was some fantasy that I was subconsciously living. Tiger brought out several stacks of jackets; including the traditional warden's red jacket that was the department's well-known trademark. There were several other jackets and parkas, including a blue dress blouse along with several other clothing items. And this was just the beginning! There were hats, boots, shoes, and several types of outdoor footwear. The pile of goodies was growing with each trip Tiger made. I felt like a winning contestant on one of those popular television game shows. The only difference being that this show was just starting and I already felt as though I was the BIGGEST winner of them all.

Tiger said, "There is a cruiser sitting out there in the yard that is yours. It previously belonged to Warden Olin Jackson but sadly Olin has a serious medical issue. It's doubtful that he'll ever come back to work for us." Tiger solemnly stated. "You'll have a boat, motor, and a trailer assigned to your district. You can pick them up at a later date," he stated. "Also there's a snow-sled here that you'll need to pick up before the fall is over," he advised. All the while he was talking, Tiger continued piling up several other items I'd need. The pile included a Smith and Wesson .38 revolver, a holster, a gun-belt, and bullets. There was a set of handcuffs, keys, and a pouch to attach to the duty belt. There were name tags, badges, compasses and a gold whistle and chain to be worn on the uniform at all times. Tiger continued bringing out sleeping bags, binoculars, flashlights, notebooks, along with all kinds of department paperwork, summons books, and a host of other items – far too many to remember. I honestly felt as if I'd been the winning contestant on "Let's make a deal."

By the time I was ready to head north, my cruiser was packed with all kinds of goodies. Goodies that most sportsmen could only dream of ever having. Once my business at the storehouse was completed, I shook hands with Tiger, and he too wished me the very best, reminding me that the area I was going to had a reputation of disliking wardens. "If you need anything, give me a shout! And good luck out there. That's a rough district you're going into," he cautiously stated.

I thanked Tiger and quickly headed off to the next leg of my journey. In Waterville, I met Dr. Sullivan for a quick physical confirming that I was indeed fit to assume my duties as a warden. The physical was more of a formality than a physical that I had been so accustomed to in the military.

Finally, by mid-afternoon, I met up with my new bosses, Warden Supervisor Charles Allen, Inspector Lee Downs and District Warden Norman Gilbert at the Burnham warden's camp. I was well acquainted with Supervisor Allen from the days when he was Verne Walker's Supervisor in Southern Maine. It was a great personal honor to think that I'd now be working for him too. The military chain of command within the warden service had yet to be implemented in 1970. In those earlier times, a Supervisor's title was the same as what a Lieutenant is today. And likewise, the Inspector title was the same as a Sergeant. Supervisor Allen, after pinning the badge onto my uniform, cordially welcomed me into the section. "Inspector Downs will be your immediate supervisor and

Warden Gilbert will be your working partner for the upcoming hunting season," Charlie stated.

We spent most of the afternoon going over mountains of paperwork, including the daily reports, summonses, warnings, and other documents that I was expected to maintain. Your position will consist of a probationary period of six months to a year," Charlie said. "During that time we'll be closely monitoring your activities to see if you are conforming to the department's policies and we'll be watching your overall job performance," he emphatically stated. He further explained that if at any time it appeared I wasn't meeting the high standards of the agency I could be let go. Having such a "black cloud" hanging over my head, was nerve racking enough to say the least, but I understood it to be a necessity for any new hire. Like Verne stated on more than one occasion, "I'd have to prove myself!"

"As for the probationary period, John. Just give it your best shot and you'll be fine," Charlie explained. "Be honest and fair with the people you serve. Do the very best you can in selling yourself and the department to these folks and you'll be just fine," he said. "The rest will take care of itself!" Charlie enthusiastically responded. "For now, just kind of poke around the area and get acclimated a bit. Hold off doing anything enforcement-wise," he cautioned. "Warden Gilbert will be working with you for a while. I have no doubt he'll help get you on the right track!" he advised.

After spending the afternoon of receiving advice, instructions, and a little familiarity with the system itself, they all piled into their cruisers and left. The big day in my life was quickly winding down. The main chore for now was trying to find a good place to eat and a place to stay for the next few nights while waiting for the Thomas family to vacate the warden's camp. One thing about it, the new district I'd inherited certainly didn't have an abundance of motels or B&Bs and restaurants. Matter of fact, it didn't have any places to stay! Max's diner was the only little restaurant located along Main Street in the town of Unity. The small diner would become my meal ticket for a while. Especially noting that cooking was not my specialty by any means. That very first night in my district I sought out every option possible, just trying to find a place to stay for the night. By now, I was ready to crash and burn. It had been a long day. In total desperation, somehow I managed to solicit a room at the fairly new environmental facility in town, Unity College. The President of the institution allowed me to share a room with a student for that first night, at a cost of $10 per night. The student didn't seem overly impressed with a game warden staying in his room, but it was the best I could come up with for immediate sleeping and bathroom accommodations.

I quickly realized this sleeping arrangement wasn't in the least a feasible option while waiting for the Thomases to vacate the warden's camp. Seeing that I was roughly making only $78 a week, I'd better be finding another place to stay. I quickly determined a mere eight dollars left over from my paycheck after a week at the college, certainly wouldn't buy many meals at the diner. Once again, whether it was luck or divine intervention, I was blessed when the next morning during breakfast at the little diner, I connected with Retired Warden Milton Scribner. "Scrib," as he was called, had been the local game warden in the area before retiring and turning the reins over to Warden Thomas a few years earlier. "Where are you staying?" he inquired.

"Right now, I don't have a place," I sheepishly sputtered. "I spent last night in Wood Hall up on the college campus, but I don't think I'll be doing that again," I chuckled. "Looks like I might be doing a little camping out," I snickered. "I'm waiting for the Burnham camp to be vacated by Warden Thomas and his family. It may be a week or two," I sputtered.

"Well you got a place now!" Scrib boldly said. "You gather up your stuff and come over to our place," he demanded. Scrib insisted that I stay with him and his wife, Virginia, for as long as I needed. "Free of charge, meals included!" he boasted. Not only did I have a great place to stay, but I had someone else with experience, like Lowell Thomas and Verne Walker, who were willing to help me in whatever way they could, as I was starting out in this young career. Scrib knew everybody in the area. Like the wardens down south, he too was highly respected by the people he served. Amazingly his wife, Virginia, reminded me so much of my own mother. She too was a diehard wildlife enthusiast, completely dedicated to the Maine Warden Service and the wildlife in the area. Virginia begged for any wild critters that might need care, should I ever run across them. "Scribby used to be bringing something home all the time," she stated. Just like my mother, she loved any wild creature her warden husband picked up that was in need of a little tender loving care. I had again been blessed to have met Scrib as I did. Staying with the Scribners was like being back home! There were times when I actually thought I was back home! And so it was on September 22, 1970, the official story of *"Living the Dream!"* started.

"You Mean He Lied to Me, an Officer of the Law?"

After moving in with the Scribners, I spent the next few days patrolling around the district with Warden Norman Gilbert. Norman was a veteran officer with many years of experience who came from the town of Hartland. Norman and I patrolled over the district's boundaries, as he pointed out the geographical area I'd be responsible for, 24 hours a day, six days a week. All told, there were sections of 16 towns I'd be responsible for patrolling. I later learned the old critter had pawned of a few areas of his own district to this rookie warden. Places he disliked having to respond to.

The Burnham district encompassed the jurisdictions of four counties; Kennebec, Somerset, Penobscot and Waldo. Warden Gilbert carefully explained how imperative it was, that any violations requiring a court action had to be brought before the legal jurisdiction of the county where the violation occurred. It was important that I knew exactly where the violation occurred and in what court the offense would be adjudicated. Trying to fully understand and interpret these necessary legalities, along with nightly periods of brushing up on the hunting and trapping laws was personally a bit overwhelming. Especially when I barely knew what town I was in, let alone trying to figure out what county.

Norman and I worked night hunters together in the evenings, but during the day I was out on my own, attempting to become better acclimated to the patrol district. I was anxiously anticipating the upcoming hunting and trapping seasons that were due to start in a few days, especially the fall trapping season. I was trying to familiarize myself with the many rules and regulations I'd be enforcing as I read through the official rule book every night just prior to going to bed. My knowledge of trapping and its many techniques was extremely limited at best. I was about as informed about the art of trapping as I'd been if someone had asked me to suddenly take over the controls of a 747 during mid-flight. In other words, I knew absolutely nothing about either activity. Other than recognizing a leg-hold trap and a Conibear trap, I had diddly-squat knowledge about the techniques of the sport of trapping. Any experience I was about to achieve would have to come from more of that on-the-job training.

However, the first valuable lesson I gained from a trapping encounter was one where I quickly was introduced to the fact that not all of the trappers I'd meet were completely honest. An incident happened one day as I was cruising out through the wooded country of Troy, still learning the roads and where they lead to. I happened to have been on an old tote road, seeing where it would lead me. As I was cruising along, I stumbled upon one of these dishonest trapping souls and never realized how dishonest he'd been until long after we'd parted company. As I slowly patrolled down an old woods road that a skidder hadn't been over for years, I was surprised to find an abandoned vehicle parked directly in front of me. The vehicle was completely blocking the roadway. The driver's side door was wide open and no one appeared to be around.

As I pulled in behind the vehicle, I noticed a man in the woods quickly scurrying my way. He was carrying a 220 Conibear trap in his hand. At that moment, I didn't have a clue what type of trap he was holding, but I knew it was a trap. The 220 Conibear trap, is a killer-type trap designed mostly to catch fisher. A fisher, just like Fritzi, that little ball of fur that used to sleep on my pillow at night! When it snaps shut, it quickly breaks the animal's neck as they pass through the spring-loaded jaws in pursuit of a well-placed meal located on the other side of the contraption. Usually, a dead chicken or other meaty substitute, secured to a slanted tree just above where the trap was placed, would draw the hungry fisher into the area. The trapping season was due to legally begin in a few more weeks. I was curious why this man was out here in the back country carrying a trap in his hand.

Having been on the job for less than a week, the trust I'd placed in the sportsman was yet to be tried. Simply stated, I was extremely naive to think someone would actually lie to an officer of the law. Especially me! What a rude awakening I was about to receive. I closely watched the man who I'll call Jimbo, calmly strolling back to his vehicle, clutching the trap firmly in his right hand.

"Whatcha' doing?" I inquired, as the man placed the device inside his car. Rather nervously, Jimbo responded, "Ahhhh, nothing really! I lost this trap last fall and I just now found it," he sheepishly responded. "I happened to think the other day of where I might have left it last year, so I decided to come out here looking for it," he stated. "I wanted to be ready for the trapping season when it opens a few weeks from now," he nervously stuttered.

He seemed to be extremely nervous and uptight for a man who had simply lost his trap from the year before. But to a rooky like myself, his answer seemed to be a reasonable enough response to suit me, as I rather stupidly said, "Gee, you were lucky to find it huh?"

"Oh yeah, he said. I was really lucky." There seemed to be an immediate expression of relief on his face, once he realized that I'd somewhat bought into his alibi. I accepted his explanation and wasn't about to question it any more. We talked for a few minutes, as I proudly introduced myself as being the new game warden in the area. Jimbo acted as though he was extremely glad to see me - and even more so, he appeared to be extremely glad when I left!

Later that evening, I related to Scrib of my brief encounter with Jimbo. Scrib quickly sat up in his easy chair, demanding to hear everything about the encounter I had with Jimbo. "You relate to me, step by step, how that transaction all came about," he barked. "Describe every detail of your little conversation with

Jimbo!" he inquired. Once I repeated the facts, a big smile came across Scrib's face, "You've been seriously hoodwinked by old Jimbo, John boy," he chuckled. "The man gotcha and he gotcha good!" Scrib snickered. "I personally know Jimbo quite well. So does everyone else in this area," he explained. "That man is a real snake when it comes to fish and game," Scrib boldly stated. "In my book, he's about as honest as Al Capone was back in his hay-day," he laughed. "Lost his trap last year, my arse," Scrib loudly chuckled. "He was illegally just setting those traps when you came along John boy, and you had him dead to rights," he snickered. "Mark my words, everybody in town will hear about Jimbo making a fool out of you in no time short," Scrib laughed. "That's his style, you mark my words John, old Jimbo made a fool out of you today!" he snickered. "He is going to make sure everyone knows it! You just wait!"

I felt as if I'd just been drop-kicked in the groin. "You mean to say he lied to me, Scrib?" I rather pathetically asked. "No one ever lies to an officer of the law, do they? No one," I muttered, while trying to justify in my own mind that I hadn't been made out to be a fool by the bastard. My worst fears came true a few days later, when a close buddy of Jimbo's stated, "John, I hate to tell you this but Jimbo's at work telling everybody about what a dummy this new warden is," he stated. "He's laughing about outsmarting you! You do know that he lied to you in regards to a trap he was about to set just when you came along," he chuckled. I could feel the blood curdling in my veins. Not so much for the well-deserved ribbing and hassling I might receive from those around town, but more so, for being so damned stupid in the first place. It was a good lesson learned. Suddenly, that sacred trust I'd placed in my fellow sportsman, was no longer there. I vowed that never again would I ever be so damn gullible. Especially when finding someone in such a compromising situation such as this one was. I was kicking my own tail, wondering how I possibly could have been so stupid. That wasn't Jimbo's fault, this stupidity and trust of a fellow sportsman was totally mine and I owned it. Deservedly so I might say.

But the incident immediately placed Jimbo at the top of my most-wanted list. Time was on my side. As Verne Walker stated in his many words of wisdom as I was heading off on my new career, "Time is on your side, John. If these people are habitual poachers, you'll run across them again and again," he boldly stated. And he was spot on with his well-meaning statement! Sooner or later I'd get my chance to repay old Jimbo for his act of deceit.

By now, this particular incident heightened my interest in quickly learning all that I possibly could about this trapping sport. It actually became a personal priority. Scrib made sure I knew what to look for, where to look for it, and many other little tidbits of the trade that proved to be invaluable in the upcoming trapping season. A season that was legally about to begin. I spent the next few days cruising Jimbo's neighborhood, searching for more traps, or signs of illegal activity. I felt as if I was on an Easter egg hunt, searching for the grand prize. Amazingly, I managed to find 3 Conibear traps, just like the one Jimbo carried out of the woods, thanks to Scrib's welcomed advice and guidance as to what I should be looking for. There were no names secured upon any of these traps as required by law. The season had yet to start, so I simply sprung them one by one, seizing them on behalf of the state. I'm not saying the unlabeled and illegally set traps I found belonged to Jimbo, but then again, I'm not saying they didn't. One thing for sure, by day's end they belonged to the fish and game department. Jimbo worked locally at the chicken hatchery in Unity. Amazingly, every one of these traps had been baited with white chickens precariously placed upon slanted trees just above the anchored Conibear trap. Although the circumstances appeared to point towards Jimbo's activities, there just wasn't enough evidence to officially charge the man. The last thing I would ever want to do, is to overreact and falsely charge a person for doing something illegal and not be able to prove it. I simply filed the facts away in my mind. I'd patiently wait for that chance to seek revenge. Like Verne had advised much earlier, "If they are indeed a poacher, you'll get your chance of revenge eventually! Time is on your side!"

And he was exactly right! The cat and mouse game was on! You can bet your sweet-bippy, that after my humiliating experience with Jimbo, I was definitely on the hunt for more illegal traps and especially for any traps around his area. It was then when I began receiving valuable information from a few other trappers who I happened to have met once the season officially opened. Trappers who appeared to be quite appreciative of the fact that I was actually giving their sport a little attention. In reality, later on in time, I found out that many of those providing the anonymous information against a fellow competitor, were themselves a bit questionable in some of their own activities.

Jimbo hadn't been the only one with traps set out long before the season opened. From what I heard he apparently had plenty of company! In the early 1970s, several trappers in the area were actively pursuing fisher. Why wouldn't they, after all a good female pelt back in those days was providing a handsome profit of upwards to $300 or more. And the area seemed to have an abundance of fisher. At the end of the trapping season, in order for the trappers to sell their furs they were legally required to present each hide to the area warden for inspection. The pelt had to be tagged with a non-removable metal seal and the catch recorded for the biologist's information. These stats were helpful in determining future seasons and limits in order to prevent the animal from being over harvested and possibly becoming extinct.

Jimbo and I would have yet another chance meeting at the end of the trapping season, when it came time for him to present his furs for registration. That is, if he had any! I really looked forward to that meeting. I intended to be just as professional and calm as possible, while at the same time, I wanted him to realize that I was aware of his unfavorable comments as to my own stupidity a few weeks earlier. I wanted him to depart my residence with the knowledge that I intended to be closely monitoring his activities from that point forward. Even though, with everything else going on, such a threat was highly improbable. And now in addition to answering complaints, checking hunters and working nights, it was my job, dealing with the sportsmen who were harvesting these fur-bearing creatures, making sure they did so, as required by law. Having dealt with Jimbo and the other trappers who were trapping fisher within the district, always reminded me of Fritzi, that little bundle of fur that used to sleep on my pillow at night.

Fritzi and I were inseparable. As I stated earlier we had a relationship between us that was similar to a youngster and his

faithful dog. As a warden, it was difficult letting go of the emotional issues of having lived amongst so many of these wild animals that had become pets – the very same species of wild animals that I'd now be watching these sportsmen harvesting. I found myself remembering the scores of raccoons we'd raised over the years and the many hours of sheer entertainment that they provided. There were so many of them, Fritzi the fisher, or Molly the otter, Bucky and Dolly the whitetail deer, and so many other wild critters, each of them leaving a lasting impression of their own.

Not wanting to get too far ahead of myself, but today as I travel around the state speaking to various groups and social organizations, recalling those many great memories and adventures of my warden's career, invariably I find myself recalling those pleasant memories of Fritzi the fisher. I enjoy sharing with the audience what it was like to have a pet fisher. Especially describing that trusting bond that we seemingly shared between us. I considered myself very fortunate. After all, how many young folks of my age could brag about having a pet fisher sleeping on their pillow at night, or playfully chasing them around the dooryard? But on second thought, how many would want to? As I share those memories with the audience, without fail, someone in the audience would ask, "What the heck is a fisher? Is it some type of an animal that fishes, or some other kind of a wild creature that has something to do with fishing?" they'd politely inquire. I was amazed at how many folks had no idea that there were fisher roaming throughout our woodlands. I quickly explained how the fisher is found only in North America. It's a member of the weasel family, similar to that of a marten, only a little larger. Their primary prey includes rabbits, squirrels, mice, shrews, and porcupines. Often the fisher is accused of killing house cats, although I highly doubt this activity is as commonplace as folks are led to believe. Not to say they haven't seized a house cat on occasion! I'm sure that when the fisher is desperate and extremely hungry that it will take a cat! I like to point out to the audience, the fact that there are very few predators capable of killing and eating a porcupine. But the fisher is very capable of doing just that. They are extremely quick and agile, unlike the porcupine who is just the opposite, extremely slow and pokey! By repeatedly biting and scratching at the porcupine's face and throat, the fisher's quick and vicious attacks eventually cause the porcupine to weaken and bleed to death. The slow movement of the "quill pig" is no match for a fisher that is running circles around them. Because the porcupine is covered in quills, the fisher then proceeds to eat the porcupine by flipping the dead or weakened animal over onto its back. It then enters the "porky" through the stomach area, where there are no quills to interfere with the evening meal. The agile fisher accomplishes this dastardly kill in extremely quick and swift motions. More than likely, the porcupine never knew what hit him!

Fritzi and I spent countless hours playing outside our rural country home, running and chasing each other around. It was like being involved in an endless game of tag which Fritzi seemed to enjoy much more than I did. The little bugger was capable of jumping from the ground, landing squarely on my shoulders, as we played for hours on end out in our backyard. Today those pleasant memories of my pal Fritzi are still priceless.

Now as a new warden, I find myself dealing with the folks who are trying to make a financial gain from trapping these very same species of wild critters I grew up with. The countless raccoons, the fisher, the bobcat and the otter, they all were fair game for the taking to the trapper who was seeking their pelts in order to make a living. With the price of pelts so high in the early 70s, I learned rather quickly that the trapping activity within my new patrol area was more common than I would have thought. I also, rather innocently, learned that not all of the trappers were abiding by the rules of the game. I have to admit that I found this trapping experience rather challenging within itself. But once I caught onto their methods and tactics, I found myself thoroughly enjoying the efforts. I invite you to come along with me on a journey into the game warden's world of competitive trapping. A world where I found that friends would "rat-out" their own friends and neighbors in their search for greed and securing an area of the sport for themselves. This activity was a personal eye-opener for a young rookie like myself, as to how the trapping world was not always the law-abiding effort I expected it to be. A few bad apples could quickly ruin the honest and law-abiding efforts of those who were playing by the rules. Rules which for the most part, the trappers in my district were adhering to. Personal greed and a sense of territorial turf struggles certainly were reasons why the game warden's job entered the picture – especially searching for those who ignored the lawful rules of the game. I was somewhat amazed at how some of my newly-found trapping friends would "rat-out" their buddies for an illegal act or two, only to have that same buddy turn upon others who they knew were violating their own activities. Once the gig was up there was no loyalty amongst competitors, it was like working inside a revolving door. When they suddenly found themselves being held accountable for some illegal action, they wanted me to know that they weren't the only ones out there who were committing a crime. There really was no honor or loyalty amongst those trappers. For a rookie like myself, it was a learning experience. Those trapping memories all started with my earlier encounter with Jimbo, a few weeks before the trapping season legally started, and at a time when I was as green as they come. And there was so much more that I would get to see as time moved on.

Again, I want to reiterate the fact that for the most part these sportsmen were as honest as the day was long. It was just those few bad apples who strayed off onto their own, who were capable of giving the sport its bad blemish. Getting back to that earlier encounter with Jimbo, Scrib was absolutely right – Jimbo was a snake in disguise. He certainly took a great deal of pleasure in making himself look extremely smart, while on the other hand, he enjoyed making his local warden look extremely foolish. I certainly learned this fact first hand! But in recalling the wise words of my stepfather, Warden Verne Walker, there would be a day of reckoning, if I was just willing to give it a chance and if I had the patience. For now, time was on my side, and I had at least 20 more years to go. My little run-in with Jimbo would certainly not be the last.

The Albino Fisher

At the conclusion of the first trapping season in my new profession, all of the trappers were required to present their hides to the local warden for inspection to be tagged and documented before they could legally sell their hides to the competitive fur buyers. This tagging requirement enabled the fish and game department to maintain accurate records regarding the harvesting of fisher, fox, raccoon, beaver, otter and other wild animals taken throughout the state. It also allowed the department to monitor and regulate the future trapping seasons and harvests.

As I began my career, I recall tagging anywhere from 70 – 90 fisher a year. At that time, a good female fisher pelt was selling for a whopping three to four hundred dollars each. Raccoon, fox, otter, and many other fur-bearing hides were also selling for a handsome profit. For those trappers within the district, the time involved was well worth the effort. Even for those who decided to start the season way earlier than what they were legally allowed. People like Jimbo for instance!

By the end of the 1970 trapping season, I had moved out of the Scribners' homestead and into the state-owned warden's camp located in Burnham. By now I pretty much was working by myself, with the exception of working during the night time activities when Warden Gilbert and I paired up hoping to capture a dastardly night hunter or two. At the conclusion of the trapping season, I finally received a call from Jimbo, calmly inquiring if he could bring his hides over to be tagged. Pretending as though I'd forgotten all about our first official meeting, I politely welcomed him to bring them along. Jimbo arrived with what he claimed to be 12 fisher pelts, in addition to a few fox and raccoon pelts. It appeared to have been a banner year for the s.o.b., or so he claimed.

But having already been deceived by the man once, I couldn't help but wonder just how legal the taking of these creatures had been? There was no way of proving otherwise, so I professionally went about the business as usual. As I inspected the hides one by one, snapping the non-removable metal seals permanently onto the pelts that he was handing to me, there was very little conversation. He'd take the tagged pelt and then pass along another one for my inspection. Like I said, the conversation was extremely quiet and quite minimal at best. I never mentioned our first official meeting, other than to wisely inquire, "You didn't happen to lose anymore Conibear traps this year did you, Jimbo?"

"Nope!" he muttered. "Why do you ask?"

"Oh, nothing particular, I just happened to find a few unlabeled illegal traps scattered in the woods earlier. Some were right around your neighborhood that had been set before the season officially opened and I didn't know but perhaps you might know who they belonged to? Either that, or I didn't know but maybe you had a few other traps that you might have forgotten from the year before," I smartly responded. "Although from what I observed, these traps were purposely and illegally set way earlier than they should have been." I smirked. "Amazingly, every one of them had been baited with fresh chickens." I added into the conversation. "Now as I understand it Jimbo, you work at the chicken processing plant in Unity, don't you?" I deviously inquired.

Jimbo seemed a bit agitated and maybe a might bit nervous, when he stated, "Nope, I don't know nothing about 'em!" he nervously exclaimed.

I thought to myself, "Yeah, right, Jim! You're right about one thing! You don't know nothing, PERIOD," but wisely I didn't say what was really on my mind. I recalled those other words of wisdom from Warden Verne Walker's great advice, "Don't take things you see or assume personally John. These guys are always trying to out-smart you, and in most cases,

68

they'll be quite successful," he wisely stated. "If they are habitual law breakers, then time will be on your side," he said. "Eventually they'll mess up in their devious tactics and you'll get your chance to bring them to justice. Especially when they least expect it!" Verne wisely advised.

Verne's wise comments indicating that "time was on my side" echoed through my head as I continued tagging Jimbo's pelts. By now Jimbo was being exceptionally quiet. He'd barely look at me as he passed yet another pelt for tagging. I couldn't help but wondering if my sudden off-the-wall inquiries were mentally working on him. But being the snake that Jimbo appeared to have been, he just couldn't make his connection with the new warden in the area without making yet another last ditch effort to ridicule the new guy once again. The last hide Jimbo presented for inspection was completely white and not the normal jet black pelt of a fisher. This hide was still attached to the metal stretcher used by the trappers in order to stretch and dry the hides of these critters in preparation for sale. Jimbo claimed this animal to be an albino male fisher. "A real rarity if ever there was one!" he mumbled.

Immediately, I recalled that very first meeting I had with the troll. A time when I trusted him! My instincts immediately sent up a host of red flags telling me not to trust him again. There just was something quite fishy about this one. Something that didn't appear to be quite right. "How come you've left this hide on the stretcher, Jimbo?" I calmly inquired, as I was looking the animal over in good shape.

"Oh, I wanted to make sure it was stretched and dried real good before I took it off the stretcher," he quipped. "It's a real rarity you know!" he bragged. "I think it might be worth a lot of money at the fur auction, being an albino and all," he convincingly stated. Closely scrutinizing the pelt, I quickly recognized why Jimbo wanted to leave it on the stretcher. The animal wasn't a fisher at all. Instead it was a white house cat that he'd obviously obtained from somewhere. Jimbo had taken the time to process, stretch, and skin, the critter, hoping I'd place a registration seal upon it, so he could brag once again to his buddies about pulling the wool over the rookie warden's eyes as he tried making me out to be a fool once again. What better way to prove his claim than to have the stretched cat hide permanently sealed to the wire stretcher, proving his point to those friends he supposedly had. Not this time, Jimbo! Not this time! I thought.

I felt my blood boiling as I refused to tag the white house cat. Before he left, I bluntly stated, "Just so you know Jimbo, I'm wise to your damned illegal antics. You just might want to be looking over your shoulder in the months and even the years ahead. You fooled me once, Jimbo, shame on you! You try to fool me twice and then it's shame on me," I boldly stated. As quickly as I possibly could, I sent him scurrying along his way.

From that day forward it became very obvious that Jimbo and I weren't about to become the best of buddies. I decided right then and there that it would be a long road with no turns in it. Time was on my side. Whether it was the right thing to do or not, Jimbo for my entire career became a personal pet project. I'd be donating a lot of my extra attention simply monitoring his activities as much as possible. Verne was absolutely right, "they'll try pulling the wool over your eyes every chance they can." I could still hear his remarks echoing in my head. I had to give Jimbo credit though for at least trying to pull yet another fast one. His smooth and suave mannerism was definitely a ballsy attempt on his part for sure! Jimbo's failed attempt of getting this rookie warden to tag his albino cat, was sent onto the main office as a memo of unusual and interesting field notes from the wardens in the field. The story was picked up by the nationally produced sporting magazine, *Field and Stream,* where this time the negative publicity went nationwide, exposing the deceitful intentions of the trapper who was playing games with the local warden. Like Scrib stated long before, "The man is a real snake!" By now, I had solidly confirmed my own opinion, that he indeed was a snake!

In due time there was a big day of reckoning with old Jimbo. A time when for once I'd be on the winning side in a case where karma returned and what went around, came around. Although it took years down the road before justice finally prevailed, when it did, it did big time! But that's a story for later. That old saying of, "What goes around, comes around!" held true. Although it was fifteen years in the making, a highly humbled Jimbo eventually got a great taste of his own deceitful medicine. A time during the cover of darkness, where Jimbo found out that he wasn't quite as wise and cagey as he once thought.

Missed Opportunities

During those first couple of months of my employment, I found myself burning the candle at both ends. I couldn't get enough of it! Concentrating on assuming my new duties, while trying to permanently settle into the area and desperately trying to learn the roads and the many little towns within my district was more than enough to keep myself busy. It was imperative to get all of this done as soon as possible, so that as a warden I'd effectively respond to whatever situations arose. Unfortunately, during this effort it was extremely difficult trying to dedicate a lot of time working the trappers in the area. But there are only so many hours in a day, and only so many days in a week. Dedicating a fair share of time to that effort alone would have to come during another season and at a different schedule. Realistically, I never would have given too much of a thought about enforcing the trapping regulations had it not been for that one embarrassing encounter out on a back road with the trapper called, Jimbo. As I said before, I absolutely knew nothing about the sport of trapping. But after my encounter with Jimbo, I definitely planned to get educated just as quickly as I possibly could. It was imperative to know exactly where to go and what to be looking for in order to make sure the trappers in the area were abiding by the rules of the game. But unfortunately the art of trapping would have to be filed away for the time being. Later on it would become a personal priority. I anxiously anticipated that moment when I could give trapping the full attention it deserved.

As time passed, a goodly amount of information for future enforcement came simply from listening to the trappers talking amongst themselves, when they arrived to tag their furs as required. It became quite obvious that there was very little loyalty between some long-time friends and fellow competitors who themselves were trappers. Especially when it came to keeping trade secrets regarding each other's illegal activities. One by one, as I tagged their furs, I'd hear, "Have you tagged so and so's fur yet?" as they then launched into a tirade of naming the individual they wanted me to be aware of. "You need to watch that son-of-a *****!" I'd hear. "He routinely starts trapping at the very first signs of cold weather in the fall. Way before the legal trapping season starts," they'd disgustedly sputter. "The rules don't mean nothin' to him!" they boldly stated.

Amazingly, I'd hear similar stories from more than one individual. Sometimes the information would concern the very individual who had secretly spoken to me earlier and who they themselves apparently were not above violating the rules. It became rather obvious that there were several trappers within my area who were not all that legal in their trapping efforts. While on the other hand, I found most of those arriving to tag their furs to be as honest as the day was long. All things considered, it was a personal challenge to determine just exactly who needed a little attention and those who didn't. Obviously with the fur market being as high as it was in those days, I definitely needed to be monitoring the district for those illegally set traps whenever I could find the time.

Finding that right time dedicated to a cause such as trapping or any other particular activity seemed to be scarce during what was considered as the busy fall season. The many duties and responsibilities expected from the wardens found us working both days and nights. There was no lack of things to do. It all boiled down to prioritizing which of the chores needed the most urgent attention at the moment. The busy hunting seasons for upland game birds and waterfowl along with the opening of firearm season for a variety of other wild critters, was quite enough to keep us running both day and night. All of this activity was in addition to answering the normal number of public complaints for a variety of incidents such as car/deer accidents, searching for lost people, dealing with trespassers, checking licenses, and simply monitoring the hunters' activities as much as possible. Sometimes it all seemed like being an endless task. Availability and being a presence to the sportsman was a critical asset of the warden's job if he was to be effective. There certainly were plenty of things to do and truly not enough time to do them. However, there was little doubt that a few trappers within the district were illegally getting an early start against their competitors. From what I was told, those folks placed unlabeled traps in areas where it would be easy for them to check, leaving few, if any, signs behind as to where they'd been. Just in case the traps happened to be located by someone like myself, there usually were no name tags attached to them, legally identifying who the trapper was – a violation within itself! In other words, the illegal trapper was willing to sacrifice a few traps in exchange for not receiving a court summons and

This was a typical fisher set - a #220 Conibear trap – using a rabbit as bait

losing their licenses. Once again I found myself thinking back to those earlier times when I was a kid, living in a home where racoons, fox, otter, fisher and other wild creatures provided so many great memories. It was time to make sure that those animals were being harvested according to the law.

Let me explain the methods used for fisher trapping for instance. This trapping business, as previously stated, was unfamiliar territory for this rookie warden, but one which I was anxious to learn This was a typical fisher set that I was finding - a #220 Conibear trap – using a rabbit as bait. In many instances chickens were used as bait. At the time, I was living in the chicken rearing area of our state, where it appeared as though every town had more than its fair share of chicken houses. Waldo County was nationally recognized for its poultry business.

These killer-type traps are placed on a slanted tree, covered over with boughs, so as not to be easily seen. State law required that the #220 Conibear traps had to be placed a minimum of four feet off the ground, so as not to impose a danger to anyone who might accidentally stumble into one of them, or to accidentally harm other animals that may wander into one. As the fisher smells the bait, he scampers up the tree in pursuit of an easy meal. In order to get at the bait, the animal is forced to pass through the square opening of the conibear trap, brushing against the small triggers. This in turn releases the powerful springs of the trap, instantly causing the animals death by breaking its neck.

Most of the trappers in my district were using chicken for bait, so it was hard to say where they came from. The Conibear trap is available in different sizes. The 3 most popular being the #110, the #220 and the #330. The #110 being the smallest and the #330 being the largest of the three. The size of the trap depends upon the type of fur-bearer being targeted. Below are examples of what type of Conibear trap could be used for capturing a certain fur-bearer. The #110 (5 x 5 inches in size) – mainly used for muskrat and mink. The #220 (7 x 7 inches in size) - for raccoon, and fisher. The #330 (10 x 10 inches in size) – mainly used for beaver and otter. The #330 Conibear traps are very powerful and require extreme caution while setting. In addition to the Conibear traps, there are several types of leg-hold traps. The leg-hold traps are strategically placed on the ground

The end result of a fisher caught in a Conibear trap

in areas with as little human scent as possible. Often a skunk scent or some other attractant is spread on the ground, which is used to draw an animal to the site. The leg-hold traps are not the killer type of trap, but merely designed to catch an animal by the leg, holding it in place until such time the trapper checks his trap and can dispatch the animal as part of his harvest. Leg-hold traps are generally used to catch fox, fisher, raccoon, coyote, bobcat, and a variety of other fur-bearing animals. There's a variety of different makes and brands of leg-hold traps – way too many to list. But the most common trap used for capturing fox and

An example of an unset leg-hold trap

racoons would be similar to the one shown above. After hearing so many comments about all of the illegal trapping going on within my district, I began concentrating on investigating the activity as much as possible within whatever timeframe I could spare. I found myself relying upon the confidential information I'd received from several of the trappers I'd met when tagging their furs. Once these people realized I'd actually spend a little time following up on their information, it was as though the floodgates had opened, with incoming confidential information flowing in from a wide variety of sources.

Most of this secretive information involved the shady and illegal activities of fellow trapper friends or a fellow competitor's advancement into what the informant claimed to be his own territory. Making a promise to never disclose the name of a confidential informant and keeping that promise at all costs, was a necessary commitment into building a sacred trust between the informant and the officer. I learned very quickly that without outside help and a trust from the public I served, I never would have accomplished half of what I was able to accomplish during my long career. Even with their help, I couldn't help wondering just how much more I might be missing!

Every law enforcement officer, regardless of agency, needs to establish a trusting relationship and a bond with the folks they represent. In a cloak of secrecy, a few of these informants personally directed me into areas where I should start searching for this illegal trapping activity. Areas I never would have found on my own. It was very obvious that the trapping business was a highly territorial sport, and for someone to crowd into another trapper's secret turf was grounds for an all-out war between the two. Each trapper was quick to protect his own terrain, even if it meant turning in a fellow competitor who was illegally infringing upon that self-imposed domain.

These informants wisely explained to a rookie such as I, just what clues I should be looking for whenever I entered an area in question. There was a little hesitation, relating to where a fellow trapper may have placed their traps and any other reliable information that I should have been looking for, as I patrolled throughout my district. In a few instances I was told exactly where to find an illegal set and who the set belonged to. But without a person's name secured to the trap as required by law, or some other means of proving who the trap belonged to, I really had no prosecutable case. More often than not, I found that mentally filing this information away often proved to be invaluable at a later date and time. In many of the places where I'd located an illegal set, I simply ended up pulling the trap, adding it to the collection I was gathering. These trapping cases were very hard cases to prosecute. In order to properly work a case, it required taking a lot of valuable time out of the busy fall activities to personally monitor and sit on the trap, hoping to catch the culprits in action. It was all but impossible to build a prosecutable case without putting forth a great deal of time into the effort.

The cell phones, pagers, portable radios, game cameras, and other highly technical tools that the wardens of today have available at their disposal, was completely unheard of back in our days. The technical gadgetry of today, allows the wardens a great opportunity to easily build cases without having to make that personal sacrifice of dedicating precious time toward the effort. Quite unlike that earlier era, when we wardens depended upon patience and a whole lot of time if we ever hoped to catch a trapper in the course of committing his illegal activities. After all, our specialized equipment in those days was nothing more than a brass compass, a good set of binoculars, and a service weapon. But that one creative tool that we older wardens always had, was never an issued piece of technical equipment. Instead, our specialized technique was called a whole lot of patience and perseverance and even at times, a little self-imposed ingenuity.

Sadly, the wardens of today no longer have that freedom of spending countless hours of surveillance like we did, due to the mandatory assignment of shift work of today, coupled with a constant demand of availability and accountability of their time. Even worse for us, was to suddenly be called away on some other pressing issue when we were right in the middle of putting together a good prosecutable case. Usually a judge never considered the severity of the offense and the time involved in proving that offense, consequently the fines assessed to a violator were hardly worth all of the effort placed into snagging him. Read on, as I describe some of those cases where time and perseverance rewarded a conviction or two.

A Case of Patience

After finally becoming a little more acclimated within my district, I decided to spend an early fall aggressively pursuing some of these early trapping cases. I recall a time when I was tipped off about two illegally set leg-hold traps placed in a remote section of rural woods in the town of Monroe. These traps had been set well before the legal season was to open.

Upon locating the traps, I guessed that probably without a doubt there were several others set in the area, but these two were fairly close to each other. These traps were situated in an area on top of a small hill far out into the backwoods of Monroe, Maine. The land had been cutover by loggers several years earlier, leaving a series of skidder trails where the logs had been harvested. Whoever these illegal sets belonged to, appeared to be checking them by using a motorbike as evidenced by the tracks left in the dirt on one of the main logging trails.

The old woods road leading up to this location had pretty well washed out years ago, and was totally unfit for vehicular traffic, other than by motorbikes or on foot. I was determined to dedicate some quality time sitting on them for a few days, hoping to capture those responsible in the act of tending them. There were no name tags attached to the sets as required by law. Also, it appeared as if they were not being checked every 24 hours as required by law, and obviously the season was yet to have legally opened, so that fact alone made the effort a priority. If I could catch the culprit involved, there would be at least three or more serious violations. One, for trapping in closed season. Two, for trapping with unlabeled traps and three, failure to check their traps once every 24 hours as required by statute.

As a warden I decided if I could successfully apprehend those involved and prosecute a case such as this, perhaps it would alert others in the area who might be doing the same thing, that they might want to literally be looking over their shoulders if they insisted on challenging the legal rules of the game. You never know when the long arms of the law might tap you on the shoulder!

The area where these leg-hold traps were strategically placed on the ground was located at the base of a couple of old maple trees. Each of them had been covered over with finely-sifted earth and dirt, and appeared to be free of human scent. The smell of wild animal urine was strong! The area had been sprayed with a wild animal scent, used to hopefully draw a fisher, fox or raccoon into the location. There were parts of a dead chicken nailed onto the tree, directly above the ground where these traps were set.

Upon locating the metal contraptions, I decided to spring the traps making it appear as if some type of a wild critter had been there and had outsmarted the trapper by springing his set. In the finely filtered dirt, I used my fingers, scratching and poking into the soil, making it appear as if some type of a wild critter had sprung the trap and had left his tracks in the soil. My obvious attempts at making faked animal impressions were far from being perfect, but they were better than nothing. If for some reason I didn't catch these culprits in the act, hopefully they'd simply re-set the traps, trying to catch the wild monster that had been there once before and had miraculously escaped.

That next morning, I was on the move well before daybreak. I was definitely on a mission. Hiding my cruiser in an out-of-the-way location, I quickly hiked up over the hill. I took up surveillance by crawling underneath a hemlock tree with low-hanging branches providing perfect cover. Those branches would keep me out of plain view should anyone come up the nearby woods road. It was a place where I could easily observe where both of these traps had been placed.

I spent the entire first day from sunup to sundown, passing the time by reading a couple of books and thumbing through a couple of old magazines I'd stashed away in my knapsack. When I wasn't reading or napping, I found myself whittling on a piece of dried wood I'd found on the nearby ground, just for something to do. Occasionally, I snacked on a lunch that I'd brought along. With the warm sun beating down onto my location, quite often I found myself taking a nap. In a small sort of way, I was desperately trying to catch up on some of that serious lack of sleep from working the long hours of both day and night over the past few weeks.

As I was reading my book, I suddenly was startled by a partridge scaling near head level close to my location. She landed on a stonewall a short distance away, never knowing that I was watching her every move. Perched ever so peacefully in amongst the quiet solitude of the deep woods, I enjoyed watching a couple of red squirrels curiously scampering around my feet. The longer I sat there, completely motionless, the closer they came. A sudden movement from a leg cramp and they went scampering away on a dead run, alerting all of the wild critters in the area that there was danger lurking under the hemlock tree.

I enjoyed listening to the sounds of the blue jays and a few crows shouting off in the distance. They too were communicating in their own subtle way of possible dangers lurking nearby. Once again, I realized just how lucky and blessed I was to have been *"living the dream."*

But other than spending a relaxing and restful day alone, far out in the thick woods, no one ever came near the traps. I kept telling myself, in a desperate effort to keep my confidence up, "any minute you're going to hear those motorbikes coming up over the hill!" But on this particular day, the effort was all for naught. They never came! At dusk, I carefully packed up my gear, and slowly hiked back to my cruiser, planning to return once again in the morning and do it all over again. Having a great deal of patience and a whole lot of determination was a trait I was proud of.

Early the next morning, I once again struck out for the hemlock tree that would become my daytime shelter. I was pumped up and rather enthusiastic that perhaps my mission would be more successful today. At daybreak I was back underneath the hemlock tree with my books in hand, a day's snacks in the ready and a lot more wood to whittle on if I really got bored.

I'd been in place for only a short time when I heard loud noises shuffling through the dried leaves directly behind me. I quickly focused my attention that way, wondering if perhaps someone had been following me up over the hill. Maybe I'd been wrong assuming these illegal trappers were coming into the area on motorbikes. I was intently scanning through the hemlock boughs hanging around my head, searching for whatever was making the loud noises that seemingly were headed my way. Within a matter of seconds, a doe deer and her two fawns came into plain view. They stood perfectly still, a short distance away from where I was perched. The doe apparently sensed something wasn't quite right, as her ears twitched and her tail came up. She was signaling to her offspring that they needed to be ready to flee the area in haste if she suddenly gave the warning. It was obvious the doe was scanning the area and testing the winds, trying to determine what it could be that was alerting her to some sort of impending danger.

I never moved a muscle for what seemed like several minutes, as I watched her swinging her head back and forth. Her eyes kept coming back my way, almost as if she knew I was there but she wasn't quite sure. Suddenly with a loud snort and a stomping of her right leg, they all shot off down the woods road on a dead run. She either caught a whiff of my human presence, or she simply wasn't comfortable with her surroundings. They quickly disappeared into the thick bushes located down on the other side of the woods road.

I quickly resettled back into my little den, picking up where I'd left off in the book I was reading. The day was slowly passing on by. Finally, the afternoon sun was starting to make its turn heading west. I was beginning to wonder if this day, too, was going to be yet another failed attempt. My patience admittedly was beginning to wane!

Suddenly, off in the distance I heard what sounded like motorbikes. Was it just some kids out for a joy ride out on the back road where I had hidden my cruiser, or could it possibly be the people I've been waiting for? I could feel the adrenaline creeping into my veins as I positioned myself underneath the hemlock tree, seeking the best possible view of the woods road below, scanning the area where I assumed they'd be coming from, if in fact it was them. The silence that followed was a killer. I was beginning to think that maybe my mind was playing tricks on me, falsely allowing me to hear things that really were not there.

After what seemed like an eternity, I once again heard the sounds. Only this time it was slowly coming my way. There wasn't one motorbike but, instead, there were two. My plan called for allowing them to actually stop their bikes and walk out to where the traps were placed, proving beyond any doubt that these traps were theirs. The simple fact was that two middle-aged men on trail bikes were out riding on the old woods road and had yet to establish that anything illegal had been done. If I was going to have a case, I had to catch them at, or near, the traps! That adrenaline I mentioned earlier, by now was pouring into my veins like never before. I was trying to prepare and envision in my mind what type of action to expect in the next few minutes. Would I be able to connect them to the illegal sets? Would they be receptive or uncooperative for getting caught running astray of the law, especially way out here in the backwoods where it was the two of them against the one of me? After all, no one really knew where I was at. Would it be someone I know or someone from far away, with no ties to the area?

Whatever the situation, I was about to confront it head on, trying to mentally prepare myself for whatever was about to transpire. The lead machine, a three-wheeler, was transporting a large man, with the two-wheel motorbike following along close behind. Closer and closer they came, as they cautiously crawled alongside of the washouts in the narrow woods road, heading my way. Suddenly they stopped directly in front of my perch and opposite from where the first trap was located. The larger gent said, "I'll check this one, you go ahead to check the other one!" he demanded.

The smaller gentleman quickly shot up the road to where the other trap had been placed. I watched as the big guy slowly walked through the woods heading straight for the trap that I'd sprung a few days earlier. By now I'd quietly slithered out from underneath the hemlock tree and was silently following along a few feet behind him. He never had a clue I was close by! He was staring straight ahead to where the sprung trap was laying on top of the ground. Arriving at the sight, he was intently staring down at the ground and the sprung trap, completely unaware that by now I was just a few feet behind him. As he stood there checking over the scene, he loudly muttered to himself, "What the hell? What the hell kind of a track is this?" he sputtered, as he carefully bent over the ground studying the sifted dirt and the several pointed finger marks I'd left in it.

I quickly spoke up, "They happen to be mine! I'm that wild animal who has been out here waiting for you for quite a while!" I calmly stated.

The startled expression on his face was priceless, as he turned in my direction and shouted, "Where to hell did you come from, John?" Obviously, we did know each other! That element of surprise was always a rewarding factor whenever it happened and a plan worked out as expected. I vaguely knew the man. He was someone I'd previously chatted and joked with at one of our local restaurants. I regarded him to be a decent fellow. But apparently the high prices being offered for furs in general had tempted him and his buddy to get an early start on the fall trapping season.

I obtained his trapper's license and any other information I needed for the summonses I planned to issue, as I politely asked him to pull up the trap and to meet me back at his wheeler. By then I was hiking the short distance up to where his buddy was located. It was comical as I headed out into the woods in his direction, he desperately tried to tuck himself in behind a big tree, with only his feet and a part of his belly being exposed. I comically shouted, "Okay, Robin Hood, you might want to come out from behind that tree and join your buddy and I down the road!" Rather sheepishly, he humbly came out from behind the tree, following me back to where the wheeler was located. I quickly issued summonses to both of these men for the three violations of trapping out of season, unlabeled traps, and a failure to attend traps every 24 hours as required by law. My patience and perseverance had paid off exactly as I'd hoped. I'm glad it had, because I was seriously thinking I couldn't spend much more time sitting under the hemlock tree neglecting those other duties within my district that required attention.

Perhaps, once the word spread throughout the district of how these men had been captured with their paws in the trap, no pun intended, others who might have been partaking in these types of illegal activities would heed the warning. Amazingly, whenever someone was cited for a fish and game violation, it wasn't long before the entire sporting community heard about it. This case was certainly no exception. I seriously thought that perhaps once the word of this incident circulated amongst the public, it just might deter the illegal actions of others. But as I soon found out, it really didn't!

I'll Let You in on a Secret

As a young warden, I learned a valuable lesson from dealing with some of these local trappers and the highly competitive nature and territorial turf struggles of their trade. It really was a high-stakes contest between a few of them, as they fought for bragging rights over who harvested the most furs during a season. I recall Scrib preaching one of his own personal lessons in one of our earlier chats, "There's not a hell of a lot of loyalty for each other between some of these trappers, John boy. They'll happily squeal on each other for some illegal activity in order to make themselves look more credible in your eyes. They'll make you think that their competitors are the worst bunch of illegal thieves around, when in reality, if the truth be known, they deserve a little attention themselves," he wisely advised. He was absolutely right. Hardly a trapping season ever passed when I wasn't pulled aside to hear the same old story, "I want to let you in on a little secret – but don't you dare say where it came from."

With my assurances that their secret was safe, they'd commence to "rat-out" a fellow competitor for a host of violations requiring my immediate attention. The closed season, unlabeled and unattended traps, seemed to be the two biggest issues I was told about. Either of these violations could result in the loss of traps and a loss of their rights to trap for a period of years. Thus, they knew if I were to act upon their secretive information, they possibly would be ridding themselves of a little local competition, allowing the informant to have a lot more territory to himself. It really was quite comical, listening to the sudden rush of information coming from a few of these individuals.

Once again, I want to reiterate that for the most part, the majority of trappers were very honest, respectable, and law-abiding citizens. It was my job to deal with those who were not. More than once, while citing a trapper for a violation based solely upon an informant's information, as I was writing out the court summons, he'd rather humbly sputter, "I want to let you in on a little secret, John," and then quite humorously, he'd commence spilling-the-beans on the very person who had just turned him in. It was as if there was a vicious circle and a revolving door of deceit and distrust between a few of these fellows trapping within the same areas. Territorial turf struggles, one might say!

For the most part, I really did find most of these folks to be honest, law-abiding trappers who thoroughly enjoyed their sport. If they happened upon violations that could possibly harm their sport, they'd openly relay the information to one of us wardens in order to protect the hobby they enjoyed. After all, it was during these times when there were several out-of-state organizations who wanted to ban any form of trapping whatsoever, claiming it to be inhumane and brutal.

These groups were gathering in strength and power, with the sport of trapping itself being placed under a microscope, while enduring a highly public opinion attack. I also found there were more honest people indulging in the sport than were those few individuals who for their own greed and competitive attitudes, were willing to violate the rules. I seldom worried about my dealings with the good ones, other than to occasionally meet them in the field as they were checking their trap lines or when it came time for them to tag their furs at the end of the season. Retired Warden Scribner wisely said, "whenever these folks offer you information regarding a competitor, you wanna take them seriously. You wanna follow up on it John boy, you'll be damned glad that you did. Usually when they tell you something in secrecy, they're right on the mark," he emphasized.

And so it was. Taking Scrib's words to heart, I vigorously pursued whatever information I received, invariably following it up with a summons or two, while gathering yet more valuable information along the way. It seemed to be an endless circle of tattletales I constantly found myself dealing with. Just as Scrib predicted it would be. One such case occurred early on in my career when Dwight, a trapper I'd summonsed for a few violations the year before, said "I'll let you in on a little secret, but don't you dare tell anyone where you heard it." He then commenced spilling-the-beans on a local trapper who I'll call Curly. Dwight went into great detail as to how Curly was using box traps to capture animals alive, mostly raccoons, long before the legal trapping season was scheduled to begin. "He's keeping them at his house in an empty chicken barn. He plans to skin them later in the fall once their furs prime up and they become more valuable," Dwight sputtered.

Dwight was adamant that I do my damn job by demanding that I do something about this illegal activity. According to Dwight, "Curly was the worst thief around when it came to trapping." The fact that Dwight's own illegal trapping escapades long after the season had closed, once again pointed out the ongoing deceit and the conniving minds amongst a few of these critters. As far as I was concerned, just being aware of Dwight's own illegal activities made him quite a thief himself. His self-righteous attitude as he related Curly's illegal activities certainly wasn't being done to gain credibility with the game warden. It was another one of those territorial turf struggles!

One of Dwight's relatives had already informed me that Dwight despised the very ground I walked upon, simply because I had seized so many of his illegal traps scattered over the countryside. So I quietly listened to what Dwight was now saying, keeping an open mind as to his possible reasons for telling this. Being aware of Dwight's continuing illegal actions would be something I could, and would, devote more time to later on. There certainly was no lack of issues and people in the trapping community to be looking into, in addition to the many other official duties expected of us wardens.

Although I never could prove it, that same family member who had warned me about Dwight's illegal activities, claimed Dwight had purposely booby-trapped a couple of 220 Conibear traps leaving them highly-concealed on the ground, hoping that I'd step in them. Traps that he had rigged to cause injury to the warden who'd been seizing so many of his illegally set traps in the past. Rather strategically Dwight left these booby-trapped instruments concealed on the ground, laying in an area where he figured I'd have the best chance of stepping into them.

In rigging these traps, Dwight had welded a series of finely-sharpened roofing nails all along the inner edges of the traps. His intention was to puncture a person's feet should they happen to approach a couple of other traps that he had conveniently left exposed in an open area where he knew the warden would be prone to venture. Only by the grace of God and a whole lot of luck, somehow I spotted one of these devices just before I was about to step into it. Even though I'd been warned, he certainly put a lot of thought and time into devising his plan! The sharpened nails permanently welded onto the strong jaws of the Conibear trap would certainly have caused major damage to my feet had I stepped into it.

Other than the confidential information I'd received from his family member regarding his devious intentions, I couldn't legally prove that they were Dwight's contraptions. The one I'd found certainly was lacking its owner's name. This particular family member thought Dwight's intentions had gone too far. They didn't want anyone getting hurt. "Dwight is quite disgusted that you haven't stepped in one of them yet," she stated. "You've seized quite a few of his illegal sets in the past and he is vowing to get revenge!"

I simply filed the information away for future reference, knowing that if I gave it enough time and patience, just like Jimbo, my day of reckoning would definitely come. But for now I rather reluctantly reacted to the info Dwight was providing on a fellow competitive trapper. Amazingly, his so-called confidential information was right on the mark. Apparently, Dwight despised Curly even more than he did me! Either that, or he thought Curly was invading his own sacred territory and he simply wanted to eliminate the competition.

There certainly was no honor or bonding between these two men, that was for sure. In due time, I worked Dwight's information with my partner Norman Gilbert. That assignment was quite a prize in itself! Stand by!

The Many Facets of a Warden's Job

A warden investigating trapping incidents and monitoring the activities of those trappers within their districts, is just one of the many assigned tasks we wardens dealt with in the fall. Unfortunately, like I emphasized earlier, the trapping season fell during the same time when the busy hunting season was in full swing, so any concentrated effort to enforce the trapping rules never really got the full attention it deserved.

Attempting to monitor the many trappers' activities in a warden's district in addition to the other chores we wardens were handling during that busiest time of the year, certainly was a difficult task for most of us to perform. Those trappers who were ignoring the rules, realized there were only so many hours in a day and only so much a district warden could be expected to investigate during that busy time of the year.

For that reason, the law-abiding trappers pretty well had to police their own sport by reporting incidents that needed immediate investigating. That is if their sport was to survive. Trapping already was under a vicious publicity attack as being a cruel and unworthy activity by those nationally organized extremists who wanted to ban the hobby completely. To be perfectly honest, unless a warden suddenly had a lot of free time on his hands to work these incidents along with their many other obligations, the lack of trapping enforcement pretty well left the trappers as being out on their own. They were expected to operate under the guise of the honor system! The following trapping cases are a selected few of the ones when I found the time to dedicate towards resolving a specific complaint. Most of these cases were the results of reliable information being passed along from another trapper.

In my previous books I related many of the various hunting and fishing incidents recorded in my daily diaries. But in those books, I never discussed the trapping cases I encountered over the many years of *living the dream.* Some of these incidents were humorous and then there were some that were not. As a youngster, having raised so many wildlife critters that these trappers were now profiting from, I knew I needed to separate those great memories, while recognizing that the controlled harvesting of game required in order to keep the balance of nature in line.

It was my intention in the following pages to share a few of those trapping incidents that were taken from the daily diaries. With the high prices being paid for furs at its peak, the greed of a few rebels became obvious. Had it not been for the law-abiding trappers in my district sharing a real concern for their sport, I never would have been successful in putting many of these cases together. Once again, proving the point that my mentors, retired wardens Verne Walker and Milton Scribner, had drilled into my head over and over as I was starting my career. "When people tell you something in secret, take them for their word and try your best to resolve the issue that they bring before you. If you are successful, they'll become the best set of eyes and ears that you ever had for years to come," they stated. Throughout my career of living the dream I found their advice to be absolutely right!

The Curly! Curly! Curly! Dance

On October 7, 1972, I was following up on Dwight's information, wondering if perhaps I wasn't being sent on a wild goose chase. I quickly located several of the box traps and a few ground sets scattered throughout the area as Dwight had described. These illegal sets were right where he claimed they'd be. One of the box traps actually contained a large live raccoon that was pacing back and forth in the wire cage. In order to prove a solid case against Curly, this incident was going to require a lot of patience and a whole lot of surveillance, waiting for him to come along to check the illegal sets. If I was to develop a prosecutable case, I'd have to directly connect him to the traps. This incident involved another one of those times when patience and perseverance would have to be the rule of the day. However long it would take to catch him red handed in the act of checking those traps, we had to make sure we were totally committed to the effort. These illegally-placed box traps were scattered throughout a small patch of woods, surrounded by corn fields in a remote area in the town of Thorndike.

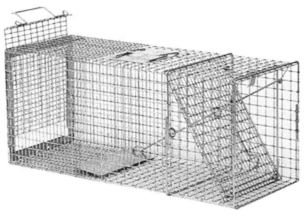

Box traps used for catching animals alive

The summer's crop of corn had already been harvested by the local farmers. The location was a perfect attraction for raccoons and fox living in the surrounding wooded area. I convinced my partner, Warden Norman Gilbert, to join me in spending a little time working the area. For the time being we'd give up our nightly excursions of attempting to catch a night hunter in order to actively pursue Curly. Should we be successful, perhaps it would send yet another message to the area trappers that we were actively giving them some of the attention needed to preserve their trapping activities. Over the next three days we arrived in a location where we would be undercover and right in amongst the mix of where all of these traps were situated. We managed to arrive at the spot every morning well before the sun came up. Both of us were committed to staying with the surveillance for as long as it took, even if it was to be a week or more. Hiding the cruiser in a place where it wouldn't be seen, we hiked up across the corn fields at 4:30 in the morning crawling into a secure spot in the woods – a place where we could overlook the entire area. We were hiding in amongst the bushes close to where these traps were placed. For the next few days we remained at this location, arriving before sun-up and not leaving until several hours later, once it started getting dark. Huddled snuggly in our warm snowmobile suits, we spent countless hours standing around in the cold, chatting about every topic imaginable, while intently peering down across the large cornfield waiting for Curly to arrive. Exercising a great deal of patience between us, we found that there were times when we both became quite bored. There was only so much one could talk about, so we took turns napping, or foolishly acting out trying to somehow entertain each other. Through all the boredom, we were thoroughly convinced that the end results would be well worth the effort involved. That is, if we could stick with the plan as we agreed. That first day slowly dragged on with no signs of Curly coming into the area to check his traps.

As the sun settled in the west later in the afternoon, we gathered up our snacks and other equipment, slowly hiking back to the cruiser, vowing to return in the morning. I couldn't help admiring the willpower and the stamina that my partner Norman was exhibiting. After all, he was 30 years older than I and he had so much farther to travel in order to get here. Norman was accustomed to having an afternoon nap during the course of his normal day on patrol. This little perk was one of those marvelous miracles we find ourselves partaking in as we age. He was quick to remind me that I was interfering with that tradition! But Norman was as enthusiastic, if not more so, about patiently waiting this one out and capturing Curly in the act. "This has to be one of the more unusual cases I've ever been involved in, John boy. Let's hope we pull it off," Norman snickered in that devious way I'd seen from the old fellow a few times before. Many of the other wardens in our division referred to the two of us as, "Grampy and the Kid!" Appropriately so, I reckon! The next day, we once again arrived real early in the morning just as the sun was rising in the eastern sky. Like the day before, we left empty handed when it began getting dark later that afternoon.

On the third trip back it was a rather cloudy and bitterly cold day for early October, as we scrambled up over the hill once more, crawling into position for yet another long day. Off in the distance it appeared as if a storm was brewing, as we huddled underneath the fir trees that were acting as our shelter. By now, and given the cold weather conditions, Norman was beginning to debate as to how long we should stay, or should we simply give up the mission, taking the traps with us and being unable to hold Curly accountable for his sins. "To hell with it," Norman disgustedly sputtered, "We've been here this long, let's at least give it another couple of hours," he reasoned. Reluctantly, I agreed, "After all, spending this much time patiently waiting, I'd hate to think we might miss the opportunity of holding Curly accountable for his illegal activities," I grumbled.

John Ford

Susie in one of her more impressive poses

We were located quite high up on a hill, with an excellent view of the surrounding area and the several houses off in the distance. The vehicle tracks left in the dirt leading up to this patch of woods appeared to be the route of travel Curly was using to check his traps. I again quickly checked the box trap holding the raccoon. A ritual I tended to each day upon our arrival. The fact that the raccoon was still there, pacing back and forth in the wire cage, established the fact that Curly hadn't been into the area while we were away. Feeling somewhat sorry for the poor masked bandit, I didn't dare bring along a small snack for the poor critter to munch on. I knew if I left a little food in the cage, and the raccoon didn't eat it, Curly could tell something wasn't just right and the mistake could be detrimental to our efforts. But I still couldn't help but think of those earlier days of my youth, back in a time when our house was often overrun with the raccoons my mother had raised. Susie, was a young female hellion of sorts that reminded me of the poor critter stuck in the box trap. Watching the raccoon pacing back and forth in the box trap reminded me of the many great times and memories we shared with those wild critters we raised so many years ago. Critters like Susie, who always seemed to find a box or some other tight place to crawl into, such as the waste can in the accompanying photo.

Now here we were as wardens, a short distance away was a young raccoon sitting on death row in a live trap, just waiting to be hauled off for an eventual slaughter by an illegal trapper who has chosen to ignore the laws. I fully intended to make sure the poor critter was released unharmed, if only my patience would last for as long as I hoped. I could have released the poor thing earlier, but I wanted to make sure not to disturb the so-called crime scene in any way. If Curly should arrive, observing him taking possession of the live coon would certainly strengthen the case being built against him.

Here we were on our third day of surveillance. After a couple of hours of nearly uncontrollable shivering and shaking in the cold temperatures, I was beginning to doubt whether or not our snowmobile suits were sufficient enough to keep us warm for this day's extremely cold conditions. The conversations between us after three days of standing in one spot, had all but ended. There wasn't a hell of a lot more we could find to talk about. Off in the distance, I noticed the visibility in the western hills appeared to be quickly disappearing. "Norman, that looks like snow coming our way," I muttered. "It can't be snow, it's only the ninth of October and it's too damned early to be getting snow," he mumbled.

But sure enough, a few minutes later, a light snow began falling upon us. The visibility was starting to deteriorate by the minute. Suddenly, Norman jumped up into the air, hoisting his snowsuit tightly up around his mid-waste as he humorously commenced to perform what was an impression of an Indian snow dance. All the while he was shouting and chanting, "Curly!

Curly! Curly!" as he was dancing and shuffling around in a small circle, placing one foot high above the other, while wildly waving his arms high up in the air. It was definitely a sight to behold, watching the old bugger pretending he was a warrior in the midst of performing an Indian rain dance! I was seriously beginning to wonder about my senior partner's mental status. Had we been standing out here in one spot for too long? I thought the old boy had completely lost his noodle, as I numbly stared at this sudden outburst of renewed energy my partner was displaying.

Chuckling as to his crazy antics, I happened to glance back down across the field just in time to see Curly's small station wagon slowly coming up over the cornfield, heading our way. "Here he comes, Norman! Here, he comes!" I anxiously shouted, as we quickly ducked in behind the branches that had been sheltering us for the past two days. "Why to hell didn't you do that stupid dance two days ago?" I sputtered, as we watched Curly slowly coming our way.

Curly drove within twenty feet of where we stood, none the wiser that we were cautiously watching his every move. He parked the vehicle along the edge of the woods, out of sight from anyone who might be coming into the area – as if there was a possibility of any traffic invading this totally remote area! Exiting the vehicle, Curly slowly lifted the tailgate, removing a couple of burlap bags from the back. Ever so nonchalantly, he strolled out into the woods heading out towards the nearby traps. Needless to say, the adrenaline was flowing into our veins like a raging river, as we patiently waited for Curly to return to his vehicle. Hopefully he'd have the live raccoon in one of the burlap bags, giving a little more credence to the information Dwight had provided, that he was taking these animals alive.

After a few minutes, Curly did return to his vehicle. As we hoped, he was carrying the bag with what appeared to be the struggling raccoon secured within it. Curly quickly opened the tailgate, tossing the thrashing animal inside the vehicle. We both slid out of the woods, just waiting for him to notice our sudden appearance. My heart was pounding, as I anticipated what kind of a reception we were about to receive. Rather loudly, I cleared my throat in order to get his attention. "Whatcha doing there, Curly?" There was nothing but dead silence, as he simply stood there with a shocked look on his face. From the blank facial expressions, he obviously knew that he was in a mess.

By this time the snow was coming down in pretty good shape. I'm quite sure that when Curly left home earlier that morning, he never dreamed he'd be having a confrontation with two game wardens. Especially on such a foul day as to what this one was turning into. Honestly speaking, I didn't expect much to happen this day either. I seriously doubt we'd have stayed in the area much longer, especially now that a blanket of snow was encompassing the entire countryside.

The timing for us had been perfect – for Curly, not quite so good! I contribute this great moment to the happenings of Norman's Curly dance! You really had to have been there because it indeed was quite a sight to behold! I quickly removed the raccoon from inside of his vehicle, releasing it back into the wilderness where it belonged. Curly had very little to say, as he was read his Miranda rights. The next few minutes were spent making out the several court summonses for Curly, charging him with a variety of trapping violations. With nothing more than a fistful of paperwork in his hands, Curly humbly left the area awaiting his day in court for later on.

Norman and I spent the next couple of hours gathering up the several traps scattered over the area, seizing them as evidence. But before finally departing the scene, Curly sheepishly inquired, "Can I let you fellows in on a little secret? Something you didn't hear from me," he humbly stated.

"What's that?" I calmly said.

"Do you know that so and so is.........how come he never gets caught for all the illegal things he does?" and thus the saga continued.

Like the times before, we now had another trapper to be on the lookout for. Once again, I recalled Scrib's wise words of wisdom, "Whenever they offer you information regarding a competitor John boy, you wanna take them seriously."

Curly eventually paid a fine for his illegal activities and his trapping license was suspended for a year or two. The fine was excessively light, $100 total for the four charges against him. Considering the number of hours we spent working the case, the effort was hardly worth the time involved. But the loss of his trapping license was the kicker that would keep him from trapping for a while. Much to the satisfaction of Dwight and a few other trappers who had been fully aware of his illegal activities, the rumor mill was quite busy over the next few days. There were many congratulatory messages from the honest trappers in the area who seemed pleased that we wardens were in fact actually able to devote a little time to monitoring their activities. For some reason, trying to convince a judge as to the seriousness of this type of activity was like trying to convince a drunk to stop drinking. They simply would not consider the time and effort required to prosecute a case, nor did they seem to care. Justice had no monetary guides, but at least in this case, justice was done!

A Rather Unusual and Dangerous Trap

I truly enjoyed taking the spare time of pounding around in the woods, searching for any signs of illegal activities that may be occurring within the district. As I look back upon those times, I was reminded of a couple of the strange incidents involving people who appeared to be in pursuit of wild animals. There were a few rather unusual trapping modes of operation that I found myself scouting for. One particular incident was brought to my attention when I happened to meet up with a young Unity College student. This student was hiking out through the thick woods near where the small college campus was located. As he walked along a narrow game trail, he happened to notice a wire draped across the pathway in front of him. Curious and cautious as to what the wire was used for, the closer he got to its location he noticed that someone had placed a set-gun secured on a homemade tripod and anchored firmly to the butt of a tree.

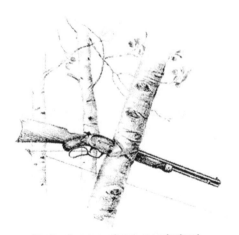

A trapper's set-gun, hammer cocked and trigger tied to a trip-line, by which a large animal 'shoots' himself.

The single-barreled twelve-gauge shotgun was resting knee high to where a normal person would be walking. Such a contraption was highly illegal and extremely dangerous to any hiker who innocently happened to be cruising through the area. Apparently, this set-gun was intended to disable one of the many deer that appeared to have been using the heavily-traveled animal path.

A short distance away from where the set-gun had been resting was an old grown up apple orchard – a place where the deer had been feeding with some regularity. By the time I was able to connect with the young college student and we returned to the scene, all that remained was the wire laying on the ground and the homemade tripod that had been securing the weapon he had described. Needless to say, this was a dangerous situation for the safety of anyone who happened to be venturing out into the area totally oblivious of their surroundings. The possibility of other similar contraptions scattered throughout the countryside was a real concern. I met with the security folks at the college, asking them to alert their students of the situation making them aware of their surroundings, should they wander off of the campus and into the nearby woods.

Fortunately, this alert student hadn't tripped the wire draped across the trail. Had the firearm worked as planned if he walked into the tripwire, the blast would have taken him knee high. More than likely he would have bled to death before being found. Warden Safety Hunter Officer, John Marsh, was quickly apprised of the situation. Over the next few days we both scoured the woods in that area, looking for any signs or evidence as to who could have been involved in placing such a dangerous weapon across the game trail. Luckily no one was injured, or worse, killed.

Never again did I run across such a weird and dangerous scenario. Several months later, one of the college students contacted the college security people, informing them it was one of their own students who claimed to have owned the illegal contraption. But there was no way to prove the case and no charges were ever filed.

Springing the Trap

Just prior to the start of the 1972 hunting season I married the love of my life. As a new bride, Mrs. Ford was quickly indoctrinated into the many hours away from home a warden was expected to work during the busy fall hunting season. On top of that, the warden's wife was expected to be her husband's messenger with every call and complaint coming through their home. She received no pay, nor praise, for the efforts she put forth. But then again, the wives never expected it. It was an accepted part of the routine. The fall hunting season was the busiest time of the year. There were many mornings when we simply met on the doorstep. Judy would be just heading off to work and I was just coming in for a couple of hours of desperately-needed shut-eye. For the most part Judy fully understood the call of duty and she was extremely supportive of my efforts. The fact that her father was a Deputy Sheriff for the Waldo County Sheriff's office helped. She too had lived those sometimes chaotic hours and the disruptive demands made upon a law enforcement officer and his family. I sometimes think the warden's job was harder on the wardens' wives and family, than it was on the officer. After all, the officer was paid for what he was doing while she never received a dime for all of her worries and stresses.

She was expected to answer the constant flow of phone calls and deal with the public complaints. Then there were a few times when she wondered when she'd ever get to see and be with her husband again. There was no doubt about it, the wardens' wives were the real heroes of the agency!

The fall hunting season required us wardens to work countless hours, both day and night, monitoring the activities within our busy districts. Daytime was spent checking the influx of hunters coming from all over the country, making sure they were abiding by all the rules and regulations and trying to keep them in line. Usually after a short break for supper, it was back out again, watching some remote field for night hunting activity. On November 7 and 8, 1972, I'd spent several hours working with Lt. John Marsh and Warden Langdon Chandler, cruising the area, running from one illegal fiasco to another. The deer season had just begun and we found ourselves scurrying about the region answering several complaints, checking hunters, seizing illegally-harvested deer and simply going from one fiasco to another. What little rest we did manage to get was from an occasional catnap inside the car, between the several episodes of illegalities being committed by a few unruly members of the gun-toting public.

It had been an exceptionally busy time, as we had apprehended a couple of night hunters, made a few arrests, and issued several summonses for a variety of hunting violations. In the process, we had confiscated seven illegally shot deer. Deer that were now strung across the lieutenant's car. His cruiser looked like a loaded-down meat wagon heading off to the slaughterhouse with all of those deer tied on top of it.

After nearly 30 straight hours of constant running, John and Langdon decided to call it quits. We all were completely exhausted. Unfortunately, as badly as I wanted to, I couldn't join them. I still had one more mission to go on.

Earlier in the day, I'd met up with a couple of young warden recruits from the area, Jim Ross and Gary Parsons from Unity. They rather excitedly described finding an illegal jungle-type snare located way out in the woods. This contraption was located behind a hunting camp in the town of Troy. The camp was owned by a group of non-resident hunters from Smithfield, Rhode Island, and it certainly was located well off the beaten path. Gary and Jim had been bird hunting earlier behind the camp when they stumbled upon what they claimed was a rope snare set on the ground, designed to snag a deer. Jim said, "You gotta see this thing, John! I've never seen anything like it before. It's a large rope net spread across a deer trail. The top of the net has been baited with apples, some type of grain, and soaked in molasses," he sputtered. "Attached to the net are a series of ropes and pulleys that are connected to a couple of wooden platforms located high up in the trees. These platforms are secured on hinges and have big rocks tied with ropes connected to them," he stated. "Supposedly if a deer walks into the wire trip that they've placed across that deer trail, it causes the platforms to collapse, springing the net up around the deer, holding it captive until they can get there," he anxiously explained.

I was trying to envision just exactly what kind of a wild contraption he was describing, but I couldn't seem to make a connection. Being in that tired state of mind, nothing at this point made a whole lot of sense. Adding to the confusion, Gary chirped, "This thing has a string of monofilament fish line running back up through the woods and into the camp. The fish line is connected through a series of screw eyes they've hooked into the trees," he added. "If anything trips the net, it's an elaborate alarm, alerting the hunters that something's entangled in their net," he explained.

"How to hell do you know that?" I calmly inquired.

"Cause we set it off and they came a running," he excitedly shouted. "We sure got the hell outta there some quick!" he laughed. Listening to the boys relate their story, it all seemed like a trumped up jungle adventure to me, and I just couldn't fathom something like that being set in the woods of Troy, Maine. I still couldn't picture exactly what kind of a contraption this might be, but obviously as excited as the boys were, the least I could do was to investigate the matter. After all, these two young men, both of them desiring to pursue a warden's career of their own, had been some of the best sources of information and help I ever could have asked for as I was embarking upon my young career. I knew from experience, whenever they told me something, they usually were spot on with their information and

I could trust them just as well as any of the wardens and police officers that I knew.

We agreed to meet at 2 a.m. in downtown Unity where together we'd sneak in behind the camp so I could see first-hand exactly what it was they were describing. I reckoned that certainly by 2 a.m. any hunters inside the camp would be sound asleep, thus narrowing our chances of getting caught sneaking around their buildings scouting out this so-called jungle net.

John Marsh and Langdon both were well aware of my last duty promise. They were having a good time poking fun of my upcoming expedition, as they dropped me off at my cruiser. John assumed I was about to go on some type of a wild goose chase and they were too tired to want to tag along. Instead, they were heading home to a nice warm bed and some of that much-needed rest that we all needed. I wished I could have been doing the same, but I'd promised the boys I'd meet them in Unity and I intended to follow up on that promise. "Don't get your foot caught in that trap you are heading for," John Marsh snickered as he sped off out of town, heading for home and that nice warm bed. A few minutes later he wisely contacted me on the radio, "John, I just saw a bent-over telephone pole alongside of the main highway down here a short distance, you don't suppose that might be some sort of a wild animal snare," he loudly chuckled. Knowing John as being the prankster he was, I could envision him snickering as he continued taunting me about my upcoming mission, while he was so conveniently headed the other way.

Little did I expect at the time, but in a few short hours the last laugh would be mine! I told the boys we would meet at the Unity Phone Company parking lot at roughly two o'clock in the morning. I wasn't really expecting too much to come from all of this, but at least I'd get a chance to see just exactly what kind of a contraption it was that they were so excitedly talking about. Besides, their prior information had always been "spot on" and I didn't want them to think I'd lost interest in what they were reporting. Being completely exhausted from the previous two days of steady patrolling, I still couldn't seem to comprehend what kind of a snare it was that they were describing.

I had an hour or so before our prearranged meeting. It was a perfect chance where I could cuddle up inside my cruiser, grabbing a little shut-eye while awaiting my faithful recruits. It seemed as though I'd just barely gone to sleep when they were pounding on my cruiser window, anxiously anticipating what the next few hours might bring. I was barely awake, as they both piled into my cruiser. Together we headed off to Troy and onto the narrow dirt road leading into where this remote hunting camp was situated. Not wanting to alert anyone of our presence in the area, I parked in a gravel pit quite some distance away from the hunting camp.

Quietly and without the aid of our flashlights, we hiked the rest of the way to where the camp was situated. Slowly we were sneaking along the old tote road, allowing our eyes to adjust to the black of night as best they could. In no time the silhouette of the darkened hunting camp came into view. Wood smoke was pouring out of the chimney indicating that the camp indeed was occupied. As we cautiously hiked up to the backside of the camp, I whispered to Gary, "Where to heck is this thing located?"

"Damned if I know! he whispered. "It all looks much different in the dark. But believe me, if you step in it, you'll know it," he mumbled.

"Oh, that's great, just great!" I sputtered. "Here we are, wallowing around in the pitch black of night, knowing this damn thing is supposedly out here somewhere, but now we don't know where!" I disgustedly grumbled.

The elaborate alarm system, leading from the net down in the woods to inside the hunting camp

"If you can get close enough to the camp, just look for the fishing line coming out through the back of the window. Perhaps, we can follow it directly back to the net from there," Jimmy piped up.

I'll be darned, good idea! "Jim, the little critter, was sharper than what I sometimes gave him credit for," I thought to myself. I made the boys stay away from the camp, as I quietly hiked up to the window, searching for the fishing line that they had described. Low and behold, there it was! A thin strand of monofilament fishing line coming out through the partially opened kitchen window. We slowly and quietly began tracing it back through the woods to where they claimed this net was spread onto the ground.

I walked away from the camp, gently holding the fishing line in my hand so as not to make any noise inside the camp. My two cronies were following along, close behind. "You really want to watch out John boy. You don't want to step into that thing," Jimmy cautiously warned.

"It's bad enough, getting batted upside the head by these damned low-hanging branches, without fearing that at any moment I might be hanging upside down from one of these trees, all tangled up inside of some damned old rope net!" I thought to myself.

We'd gone a short distance when suddenly we arrived at where this large roped netting had been strategically spread across the ground. Fortunately for us, the fishing line led me directly to a small plywood platform placed high up in the nearby tree that was firmly holding a large boulder secured onto the platform by ropes and pulleys. The ropes were connected to a series of well-placed pulleys that eventually were hooked onto the large net spread out on the ground. Obviously, the rocks resting on the small wooden platforms attached high up in the trees, were acting as weights designed to snap the rope net up over the deer, entangling him in the process. There was a small fir tree conveniently placed as a trip, as it lay horizontally to the deer trail at about 3 feet or less off from the ground. This elaborate setup was designed to release the big rocks, causing them to swiftly fall from their platforms caused by any large animal bumping into the intended trip. The falling rocks attached to the ropes would release from their platforms overhead, causing the net to spring up over whatever animal was caught inside the roped netting. While looking this gadgetry all over, it was kind of an archaic contraption, where hopefully the animal would be restrained just long enough for the hunters to exit the nearby camp and dispose of the animal before it could escape – thus the purpose of the fishing line alarm running back into the camp. The fishing line ran in through the kitchen window and was attached to an empty Pepsi soda can that was filled with nuts, bolts, and washers. Supposedly an animal, such as a deer, by thrashing around and caught in the net, would make the can jump up and down inside the camp's cast iron sink, alerting the occupants that there was a critter entangled in their trap. Time would certainly be of the essence in order for them to get to the animal before it escaped.

This rather elaborate setup was exactly what the boys had so eloquently described. Whether it would have been capable of accomplishing its intended mission or not, who knows? None-the-less it certainly had potential and it was illegal! I'd never before seen anything quite like it. Contemplating what course of action to take, I decided to place the boys well out of harm's way. If ever I really wished that Lt. Marsh and Warden Chandler were now standing beside me, this certainly was that time. I intended to spring the trap, hoping to draw the culprits out of the hunting camp in order to prove who it belonged to. What the heck, if they came armed with lights and guns, I'd actually bag a couple of night hunters in the process. They'd be hard pressed to say what they were doing with lights and an armed firearm running through the backwoods of Troy at such an hour of the night. If for some reason I couldn't get them to come to the trap, they easily could deny any knowledge of ownership.

Other than a circumstantial case because of the connection near their camp, I reasoned it would be much better to get them thinking they had succeeded in their efforts. Although, the fishing line leading back into their camp certainly would have made it hard for them to deny any ownership or knowledge. I'd be left with nothing more than a good circumstantial case – being unable to directly connect the responsible parties to the crime scene itself. It was show and tell time, as I ordered my two helpers, "You guys get down over that banking over there and stay put until I tell you to come out," I barked. "No matter what happens, don't make your presence known until I tell you that it's okay. Should for some reason something go sour here, you guys sneak to heck out of here and get some help!" I advised them.

I suddenly realized the potential danger involved with what I was about to do, and I now wished that they hadn't been with me. Again I thought about how much better it would've been, had Lieutenant Marsh and Warden Chandler been there protecting my back. Just to have someone else with a little more legal authority assisting my efforts would have been ideal, but it was too late to be thinking about it now. I was sure that by this time, my two warden buddies were home, snuggled warmly between the sheets, catching up on that lack of sleep they'd been deprived of over the past two days. And now, here I was, all by myself, standing out in the middle of the woods at 3 a.m. with the adrenaline rushing into my veins like never before, anticipating what the next few minutes might bring.

As I firmly grabbed onto the fishing line, it was time to test how effective this elaborate contraption would be. Once I was completely satisfied the boys were placed well out of harm's way, I began yanking and pulling on that fish line as hard as I could. At the same time, I was blatting and calling in a half-hearted attempt to imitate the sounds of a deer in distress, whatever that might have sounded like. Gary and Jimmy started laughing uncontrollably down in the bushes where they were hiding. I had to bark at them to be quiet, that this wasn't quite as funny as they were making it out to be!

I could hear the soda can clanging and banging inside the camp. The alarm system was working perfectly, just as the boy's stated it would. Within moments I could hear a stirring of activity coming from within the hunting camp. The door burst wide open, with three separate beams of light streaking down through the woods, rapidly heading my way. My heart was racing like never before, as I continued blatting and trying to imitate a deer in distress. Hiding behind a large nearby tree, I planned on letting them get much closer before making my presence known. I could barely make out the silhouette of the first man who was bounding down the trail like a jack rabbit, heading toward my location. He had a firearm grasped firmly in his hands, obviously anticipating finding a deer tangled up in the crafty-made contraption.

Once they had arrived close to where the net was placed, I screamed, "Hold it right there, gentlemen! Hold it right there! I'm a Maine Game Warden and you're all under arrest." I'm sure my voice could have been heard for miles away, as the echoing of it out through the surrounding terrain even scared me. The next few seconds grew quite intense, when the young fellow toting the shotgun quickly raised it up to his shoulder, pointing it directly at my head. Instinctively, I removed my department issued .38 caliber sidearm, as we stood a few feet apart from each other in what could have been called an armed standoff.

I kept screaming for him to drop the shotgun, while I pointed that small .38 caliber peashooter his way. One thing for sure, the weaponry I had was no match for the load of buckshot and the 12-gauge shotgun that he was carrying. In comparison, it was quite similar to sending a soldier off into battle with a slingshot and a rock, against a fully armed battalion. Sadly, I just happened to be carrying what was equivalent to the slingshot! I continued screaming at the top of my lungs for him to lay the firearm down, as I pulled a big bluff of sorts. I was yelling, "Don't be foolish! Drop the firearm. You are surrounded by other wardens," when in reality I was alone. Well I did have my little buddies hiding off to the side should something bad happen.

Tootie and Muldoon, the two warden wanna-be's, strategically were placed down over the bank, secretly watching this fiasco unfold. But realistically, the boys were unable to assist should I have needed it, other than to sneak away and render help by alerting someone of authority exactly where I was located. All three hunters were clad in their pajamas, but then again why wouldn't they be? What more could I expect, after waking them up from a sound sleep? The elder member of the group quickly convinced the young fellow to drop his shotgun and to submit to my demands. It certainly was a tense situation for a few brief moments. Moments that for me seemed like an eternity! There was no doubt, when I eventually got the chance to go back home, I just might have to perform a check of my shorts.

Once the initial shock of the unexpected law enforcement presence had sunk in with these three early-morning night hunters, they humbly submitted to the demands and were extremely cooperative from that point on. Seizing control of the weapon, I escorted the group back to the camp, where I prepared them for the long ride to the Waldo County Crowbar Hotel. As it turned out, the camp owner knew the legal process well. He just happened to have been a bail bondsman from Rhode Island. A man who was very familiar with what the legal procedures were from here on in. Ray was not the least bit envious or disgruntled as to what had transpired on this early morning. As a matter of fact, he was quite cordial and extremely humiliated as we chatted about the deer hunting and the extremely poor luck they'd been experiencing at this location over these past few years.

Ray pointed to a record they'd maintained hanging from the camp wall, documenting several years of previous hunts. The record showed that not one trophy deer had ever been taken by any of the hunters coming to the camp. I found this lack of success quite hard to believe. After all, they were located in what I considered to be some of Maine's very best deer country. Others who had been hunting in the same area, had been extremely successful. In fact, over the years, there were some big trophy bucks bagged within this same remote area of woods. Ray commented, "Well John, at least by now I hope you can see why we are so desperate to try anything," he humbly stated.

"Do you honestly think that roped rigging would ever have worked as successfully as you planned, Ray?" I calmly inquired.

"I dunno!" he said. "I learned how to make one of them several years ago when I was stationed overseas in the military. We caught a few wild critters in a net like that in some of the jungle areas where I was assigned, but you really had to respond quickly before they got out of the net and escaped," he stated. "In response to your question John, I seriously doubt we would've caught a deer," he stated. "It was a million-in-one shot, but after all this time of going home empty handed, we were ready to try just about anything," he sheepishly stated.

Once the dust had settled and the excitement of the past few moments had calmed down, I was rejoined by Gary and Jim. Ray, along with his son and nephew, were advised that we had to hike down the road to the cruiser for the long journey to the Waldo County Jail. Ray was being totally cooperative, so I allowed him to take his own vehicle and follow us the 30-plus miles to the county lockup. That way once bail was made, they'd have a means of transportation back to the hunting camp. By now the sun was starting to rise in the east. That sleepy spell I'd been experiencing earlier all of a sudden no longer existed. There was no doubt that the earlier big rush of adrenaline was now keeping me going.

Making That Call to Lt. Marsh

After booking the three detainees into the Waldo County Jail, I couldn't wait to make that crack-of-dawn call to Lt. Marsh, hopefully waking him up from a pleasant and sound sleep. Being the devious devil I was, it was time to let him know the real excitement he had missed. John Marsh, as a warden, loved to be involved in apprehending poachers and feeling that usual adrenaline rush involved in capturing folks in the act of committing a crime. Knowing him as well as I did, I knew he certainly would have loved to have been standing right next to me on this one!

His phone rang several times before I heard his groggy voice on the other end saying, "Hello - hello!"

"John boy, were you sleeping?" I sarcastically inquired. "What the hell do you think I was doing!" he rather bluntly stuttered, quickly followed by a rather irritated, "What's up?"

"Well John, I just wanted to tell you that I'm at the Waldo County Jail with three non-resident night hunters who had an illegal deer snare. I thought you might want to know all about that snare you guys were teasing me about when we last met. The boys' information was in fact, the real thing," I excitedly squawked.

"You're kidding me! Tell me you're kidding me," he disgustedly mumbled. I somehow sensed he had suddenly sprung to life, seeing how he was such a stickler for catching night hunters. More so, he simply loved being included in on the action, no matter where it was. "What happened! Tell me what happened," he begged.

I related the hair-raising event of the past few hours, as he sighed and groaned in total disgust, griping and complaining to himself for not being there. I had the last laugh on the old boy after all. Especially recalling how much enjoyment he seemed to be getting while razzing me when we departed company earlier that morning. "You haven't taken any of it down yet, have you?" he inquired, referring to the rope net.

"Not yet, I'm going back up there to get it now," I said.

"Don't take it down!" John demanded. "I'm going to call Paul Fournier, the department's photographer and we'll be heading your way to document just what you have up there. Don't you touch a thing!" he barked. "Damn it! Damn it! I wished I'd been there," He kept muttering over and over. "Aren't you tired?" he asked.

"I was earlier, but I guess I'm running on sheer adrenaline at this point," I calmly responded.

John Marsh pointing to one of the rock-loaded platforms that was attached to the rope snare

The rest of the morning was spent with Lt. Marsh and my immediate boss, Supervisor George Nash, along with a small crew of bordering wardens, as we gathered up the net while photographing the entire setup for evidentiary purposes. All the while, Lt. Marsh was shaking his head in disgust, realizing that he had passed up a golden opportunity to have been in on the action. Ray and his two cohorts were awarded the dubious distinction of being arrested for the most unusual and serious fish and game offense during that 1972 fall hunting season. Upon paying a record fine, they left the courthouse, shaking my hand with no ill feelings. As a matter of fact, I was invited back to their camp anytime I was in the area for coffee and to chat.

John Marsh holding up the net snare

"No hard feelings on this end," Ray said. "We were wrong, and we knew it. You were only doing your job," he humbly stated.

I wished all of the people I'd dealt with over the years had that same type of forgiving attitude, but unfortunately there were those who didn't. I was extremely impressed with their cooperative attitudes, an honest display of respect showing that even those sportsmen who occasionally stray over the line can be real gentlemen when they want to be.

I was finally anxious to go home and crawl between those sheets I hadn't seen for the past few days. The old body had reached its limit! After three days of continuous activity, with an occasional cat nap thrown in wherever I could get one, it was finally time to go home and hug Mrs. Ford. Thankful for having the opportunity to do so!

It was finally time to catch up on some of that desperately-needed rest. After all, these past three days of constant activity and all kinds of excitement had been quite enough for the time being. But as tired as I was, through it all I was still some thankful to have been *living the dream*! And what a dream it was!

Sometimes Things Don't Go Quite as Planned

Sometimes we wardens aren't quite as smart as we think. Especially when it comes to staying one step ahead of these people we consider to be occasional lawbreakers. People who have already established a prior record! This particular incident proved to be just such a case. I met up with another one of those highly competitive trappers who wanted to pass along a "little secret" regarding my old pal, Curly. The same Curly who Warden Norman Gilbert and I spent three days huddled together in the bushes waiting for him to tend to his illegally set box traps months ago.

As a result of Curly's prior illegal activities his trapping rights had been revoked for a year. According to my confidential informant, Curly was now preparing to trap for fisher, even though he knew his rights to do so were under suspension. Only this time he planned on staying close to home, thinking he'd be safer than when he had been caught in the past, according to my information I'd been given. I wasn't shocked to hear this news, especially seeing that I doubted the license suspension would really curtail Curly's efforts to begin with. In a humorous sort of way, I knew him to be somewhat of an independent cuss.

Curly, while being a very likable fellow in every other way, had a very stubborn and independent streak about him whenever it came to fish and game matters. He gave the impression that the wildlife laws never really met with his approval, nor did they ever apply to him. Curly wasn't alone in those thoughts however. The state certainly had more than its fair share of folks who felt the same way. But I wasn't the first warden to realize that if it wasn't for a few folks like them, we wouldn't have had a job. Their obvious disobedience is what we wardens called job security! I refused to take any of their activities personally, except of course that one time early in my career when that sleazy trapper called Jimbo caused me to violate that theory. I was still waiting for karma to come his way, although he had been quite quiet for some time. In return for treating these folks as respectfully as possible, hopefully they didn't take my actions personally, when suddenly they found themselves in some rather compromising situation. I had a job to do, and I intended to do it as fairly as possible.

The exorbitant price of furs was way too high for someone like Curly to pass up yet another year without his being able to cash in on the high prices. Someone like Curly, who was so skilled at the trapping trade, simply couldn't stop pursuing the activity just because his license to do so had been revoked. If for nothing more than the monetary rewards and his own personal greed, I assumed he'd be right back at it, license or not. My latest informant was sort of confirming that fact. I knew Curly well enough to know, if he figured he could get away with it, he'd be trapping just as he had in the past. License and be damned, it wouldn't matter.

I was advised to check a remote area in Thorndike near Curly's home, a place where I suspected he had trapped in the past. As I hiked out through the woods, I found dead chickens tacked to the bases of a few trees. It was obvious that whoever had placed them there, did so with the intent to draw fisher, fox, and raccoon into the area. I expected that within a few days, leg-hold traps would undoubtedly be placed at the base of these trees by those who had been baiting them.

It was still early October and a couple of weeks before the trapping season was due to officially open. I planned on closely monitoring these remote sites, hoping to eventually find the traps and to spend a little time working on who they belonged to. In my mind I honestly suspected Curly to be the culprit, as this place was close to being in his backyard. The mere fact that his license had been suspended made this incident a pet project - a challenge of sorts. Besides, once again, the location was off the main road and in close proximity to his home – a place where I was sure he'd feel quite safe. Access into the area was via an old tote road leading into a local farmer's back fields. It was a perfect location for the wild critters that were being sought. There was no violation for having nailed dead chicken carcasses to the sites prior to the start of the trapping season. It made perfect sense to have these animals coming to an area where they knew they could get an easy meal.

Over the next few days, I kept checking the area, thinking that perhaps Curly might have declared the season officially open. He'd be doing so under his rules and certainly not those of the department's. On each of the return trips, there still were no traps placed around these baited areas. It was very evident that some of these animals had in fact located the chickens nailed to the trees and that they now were making regular visits to the site for an easy meal. It was only a matter of time before whoever had baited the area would show up to set their traps. I was thoroughly convinced it would be Curly, but still I was highly surprised that as of yet he hadn't set the traps. Maybe he was being a little extra cautious, so as not to be charged with another closed season violation should he get caught. Although, with his license being suspended, what difference did a day or two make? The trapping season was due to officially open on October 28.

I checked the area again late in the afternoon of the 27th and like the many times before, there were no signs of any traps. I planned on hiking back into the area well before dawn the next morning, patiently waiting for Curly to arrive, even if I had to spend a day or two huddled in the brush waiting. At 3 a.m. on October 28, I hid my cruiser far away from the area so as not to let anyone know where I was. Once again heading off into the woods on foot and crawling into a spot near where these pre-baits had been set. I'd brought along plenty of items to snack upon, including a book or two to read. I knew it could be a long day or more, but in the end hopefully the effort would be well worth it.

At daybreak, I was comfortably snuggled in amongst the bushes, in a place where I could observe the tote road and an area where my friends would hopefully come diddly-bopping along. At approximately 8 a.m. I heard the crunching of gravel and the quiet purr of a car's engine slowly heading my way. Sure enough, I recognized the vehicle coming as my pal Curly's. This was going to be way too easy, I chuckled to myself. I slid underneath a low-hanging hemlock tree seeking cover, as the vehicle stopped a short distance away. Much to my surprise, Curly wasn't in it. Instead I watched as Curly's wife, Fay, and her friend, Leona, opened the back of the small station wagon. They removed a small wooden box from the rear of the vehicle, quickly disappearing into the area where one of the dead chickens had previously been placed. I thought to myself, "Surely these women wouldn't be in here setting traps. Women certainly weren't noted for their trapping efforts in my district, but what else could they be doing," I thought.

Not wanting to tip my hand, I simply waited until they returned to their car, replacing the wooden box in the back of the small sedan. I watched them slowly continuing on down the road to yet another location where a dead chicken had been left. These ladies had done absolutely nothing illegal. "Could it be they were making a test run to see if they really could flush me out of the woods in an effort to make sure the coast was clear for Curly to come in right behind them and set his traps?" I thought. I didn't want them to know the eyes of the law were watching them.

I waited until they were well out of sight before hiking over to where the chicken had been, seeing if anything had changed. This is when my own stupidity came into play. Prior to writing this story, very few people ever heard of what happened next. At the base of the tree, a fresh chicken had been carefully placed where the old one had been before. I noticed a small mound of sifted dirt freshly deposited upon the ground. Without thinking, I began to slowly brush away the silt with my hand, observing if in fact there was a trap there. Surely these women weren't capable of setting traps, I rather stupidly concluded. Suddenly, ka-snap – the jaws of a metal trap firmly latched onto my right paw. It hurt like hell, as I quickly jumped back with the jaws of the trap firmly clamped on the ends of my throbbing fingers. Suddenly, I could relate to what a wild animal must have felt like when it found itself caught in the metal jaws of one of these contraptions.

I wanted so badly to scream and swear, but I knew if I did, the women would hear the cussing. I spent the next few minutes carefully prying the metal jaws apart and off my throbbing fingers. Jaws were clamped firmly upon at least three fingers. Slowly removing one finger at a time, I quickly made sure each of them were still functioning properly. Eventually, I was able to free myself from the trap. How stupid I'd been to have put myself in such a compromising predicament. I simply stood back completely dumbfounded, staring at the disturbed sight in total disbelief. I had no idea that Fay and Leona were actually trapping, or that they even knew anything about the process. This was a definite first for my area, but looking back upon it all, Fay surely had a great teacher.

I learned a very valuable lesson the hard way, on that cool fall morning. Sometimes the mind can convince us of things that aren't always what we think they are. And sometimes the information we receive from a competitive trapper isn't always accurate. This little incident happened to be one of those times. Another lesson I learned from this foolish escapade was to never doubt a real sportsman's wife in regard to her outdoor capabilities. It's a losing proposition. Over the next few days, my throbbing fingers and sore paw could definitely avouch for this fact!

Taking a Cold-Water Plunge in Zero Degree Weather

Reviewing the pages of the diaries that I managed to keep regarding my great career, I was reminded of a bitterly cold February morning in 1977 when I headed off to check a remote beaver flowage in the town of Troy. While flying over the district the day before with my buddy, Warden Pilot Dana Toothaker, we located this beaver flowage situated well off the beaten trail. It was a newly-constructed beaver pond. One that I never knew existed!

As we circled low over the beaver pond, it was rather obvious by looking at the many set-poles surrounding the beaver house, that several trappers had become aware of this place and had converged onto the frozen beaver pond en mass. A few of these sets looked to be a bit closer to the beaver house than was legally allowed.

"There's a good chance to snag a bad guy or two down there John boy," Dana said as we scaled low over the treetops looking over the sight for one last time. There had been an unusual February thaw that year, followed by a rather hefty snowfall blanketing the region over the past few days. At times, it had been so warm it felt as though spring had prematurely arrived, but on this particular day there was no doubt that winter was back. And it was back in full force! The temperature was hovering at a minus 4 degrees with a brisk northeast wind when early that morning I departed my residence heading for the beaver pond located far out in the woods. The cold wind whistling through the trees, coupled with a light blanket of loose snow circling around in the frosty air, was typical of a normal cold, wintry February day. The wind chill was dangerously below the freezing mark, nearly taking my breath away each time I inhaled. In a strange sort of way, I found it to be quite

131

peaceful and rewarding to be outside in the cold air performing my law enforcement duties.

As I slowly hiked through the thick woods heading for the beaver flowage, I was meandering farther and farther away from my cruiser and any form of civilization. We wardens had no cell phones or portable radios available during this era. Those items were totally unheard of and hadn't yet made their grand entrance into the scheme of available law enforcement equipment.

I was thinking about the dramatic change in the climate over the past few days as I slowly shuffled along in the snow, plodding deeper and deeper down into the thick woods. Suddenly I spooked a couple of whitetails, concealed beneath a grove of Hemlock trees located adjacent to the path I was following. They quickly crashed out through the brush in an effort to place as much distance between us as possible. That's gratitude for you, I thought. Here I'd spend most of my career protecting these damn critters and now they wouldn't even hang around long enough for me to enjoy their beauty and grace. "Oh well," I sputtered, as I continued on through the woods heading for the flowage.

I was anxious to check out this newly-found location. Had it not been for the earlier flight with Dana, I never would've known the place existed. Although, the snowshoe trail heading off into the thick woods might eventually have caught my attention sooner or later as I patrolled through the area. The indication of snowshoe tracks heading out into the woods usually perked my interest, as I wondered who's they could be and where they were headed? And more importantly, I was always curious what purpose they'd taken to venture there. More often than not, I found that by following up on a human presence heading out into the woods, sometimes it would lead to a situation where folks would find themselves in trouble with the law.

As I hiked along on my snowshoes, I finally observed the large beaver flowage off in the distance. It was barely visible through the trees. There was a light layer of misty-like fog rising from the small stream flowing out of the beaver pond. The open water from the stream was apparently warmer than the cold air surrounding it, which created an eerie haze that was kind of drifting down through the woods. Thank God for the department's issued heavy parka and the wool uniforms that adequately protected us from the extreme elements on cold days such as this one. With the hood pulled securely up over my head, I was as snug as a bug-in-a-rug.

Clutching my faithful chisel in my hands, to chop away the ice from any traps I felt were in violation, I actually was enjoying the journey as I slowly trudged over the light layer of snow that had blanketed the area from the previous few days. I continued following the snowshoe tracks out onto the flowage heading to where the many set-poles were protruding high up above the ice. These poles indicated where each individual trap had been placed. Usually the trapper marked each pole with his name and a trapping license number for identification so that we wardens wouldn't chop the traps out of the ice, making sure they were legally tagged and we were able to identify who the traps belonged to. If there were no names, the traps were seized and became property of the state.

I finally reached the area in question. By now I was better than a half mile or more from my cruiser. It was definitely going to be a slow and cold uphill walk back to the cruiser, once my business was completed and once I had cleared the flowage. The huge beaver hut was completely surrounded by a large number of set-poles, indicating several trappers were seeking the furry inhabitants of the pond. As I walked in amongst these poles, I noticed that two of them seemed to be placed extremely close to the beaver house itself. They were set well within the 25-foot minimum as required by law. Actually, they appeared to be less than 8 feet from the beaver house. There was little doubt whether or not this trapper had inadvertently misread his tape measure, if in fact there were traps attached to the poles. Occasionally I learned that a devious trapper or two, would purposely stick poles into the ice near a house or beaver dam in what would appear to be a definite violation of the law, with no trap attached to the poles. A sneaky decoy of sorts to irritate a warden! This intentional act was done to draw a warden into the area, knowing that it would be a wild goose chase for the warden when in reality no laws were broken. I intended to seize the illegal sets if in fact they were there. As I hiked in amongst the many poles walking toward the beaver house, I suddenly and without any warning whatsoever, plunged straight down through the ice and into the cold water below.

I was surrounded by a maze of exceptionally strong, spring-loaded #330 Conibear traps attached to these set poles. The killer type #330 Conibear traps had to be set with brute strength, as the powerful springs were well equipped to perform the immediate killing function they were designed for. I could only imagine kicking and floundering around trying to escape the predicament I now found myself in, only to have one of these traps latch onto my snowshoes, or even worse, my legs.

It all happened so quickly. Instinctively, I quickly extended my arms and the chisel parallel to the ice, catching myself on what remained of the thicker ice around me. I was dangling almost midway to my chest in the freezing cold water, with the ice cracking from my weight. For the time being, the thin ice prevented my body from becoming completely submerged in the cold water. With snowshoes attached to both feet, it was impossible to swim if I had to. I didn't dare kick or thrash, fearing one of the large 330 Conibear traps might firmly latch onto my snowshoes, or even worse, onto my foot. If that were to happen I'd be there for the duration or until some trapper showed up to check his traps, days, if not weeks, later! The trapping laws for beaver didn't require a daily check of the traps as it did for other game species. Honestly speaking, there were certain parts of my anatomy signaling for me to get the hell out of that water as fast as I could. My deep voice suddenly changed to a high-pitched soprano, if you know what I mean. I was beginning to have serious doubts whether I was going to survive this ice-cold dunking, especially after being weighed down by those heavy wool pants and a half-soaked winter parka, all the while sporting snowshoes tightly attached to my feet. It was no time to panic, that's for sure. But even realizing that fact, just thinking about it was a lot easier said than done.

Somehow, I was able to inch myself back up onto firmer footing, all the while the thin ice continued cracking all around me. I felt warmer in the water than I did when I finally was back up on top of the ice. To panic now could result in a fatalistic ending and I was too damn young for that to happen. Besides, I had a new son and a loving wife back home that I desperately wanted to return to. I had no idea how deep this pond might be - and I really didn't care to find out.

Finally, I managed to somehow roll myself up on top of more solid ice and footing, where I briefly remained while recouping my breath and gathering up what strength I had left. The cold wind and swirling snow weren't helping any. That "snug as a bug-in-a-rug" feeling I once had no longer existed! Relieved to be back on solid footing, I knew I had to get back to my cruiser just as soon as possible. If not, I could easily fall victim to the onslaught of hypothermia, a condition that has managed to claim so many lives each year. I knew that just because I might have been a warden, I wasn't exempt from Mother Nature's wrath! My heart was pounding like a jackhammer laying on a solid slab of cement, as I managed to slowly stand up. Within seconds, my pants were turning into what seemed like solid layers of ice, making it extremely difficult to walk. And I had such a long way to go.

I quickly started backtracking along the trail, heading for my cruiser, hoping that once I was in the woods it wouldn't seem quite so cold. I was shivering uncontrollably, probably more from the excitement and the predicament I suddenly found myself in, rather than from the cold temperatures surrounding me. Scurrying up the narrow trail like a rabbit being chased by a possessive hound, I was not dilly-dallying, that's for sure. I was afraid if I were to stop, even for a short rest, I might not want to continue. Along the way, I spotted what I assumed to be those same two deer again. I swear as I watched them this time, standing there unafraid, that they seemingly had a wise smirk on their faces, as I quickly scurried on past them. This time they stood completely still, watching my sorry tail shuffling on past their location. The damn ungrateful critters! I might have to contact my old poaching buddy Grover, making him aware of where they were hanging out. "Smirk at me, you damned thankless creatures," I thought, as I scurried on past them.

Finally, off in the distance I saw my cruiser. Just the sight of it gave me a renewed burst of energy, as I made that final big push onward. My wool trousers by now were frozen solid. They were heavy, feeling as if they were coated with a layer of heavy iron. Every step along the way seemed like a never-ending chore, but before I knew it, I was unlocking the door of the cruiser and quickly climbing inside. With a huge sigh of relief, I started the engine, turned the heater on high just as far as it would go. I hastily shot down the narrow road, headed for home and some dry clothes and to take what I hoped would be the hottest shower I could stand. That warm blast of welcomed heat was starting to thaw out my face and my frozen body. The heat and warm air were just what the doctor ordered. I found myself grinning from ear to ear just like a kid with a new toy, thankful to have survived yet another ordeal out in the vast wilderness of God's wild country.

And thus it was on that cold and frosty winter day, I'd taken the plunge of a lifetime. It was an incident that I'd not soon be forgetting, as I wrote the daily notes into my diary. That Divine intervention that had been with me so many times before, had once again rescued me from what could have been a real personal tragedy.

I never did manage to return back to that beaver flowage that year. Perhaps it was that bad memory that subconsciously kept me away, but I'd more than likely think the timing was never right for a return. To this day I wonder if perhaps those poles had been purposely set too close to the beaver house, indicating that it was a violation of the laws, or perhaps it simply was a booby-trap aimed at drawing a warden onto the thin ice! If it was the latter, whoever placed those stakes where they were, certainly had pushed the limits for themselves by going onto that thin ice to set them! I'd rather think that, more than likely, the warm spell of a few days earlier allowed the ice to weaken in the area around the beaver house. There were some folks in the area who still despised the law enforcement activities of us wardens, but I doubt this would ever be one of their tricks. But once again, the only way to look at their devious rebellion is to realize how much their illegal activities provided us wardens with a real sense of what was called 'job security.'

A Few Tips and Welcomed Advice –
Follow the Tracks!

As I was just beginning my new career, I was given a variety of suggestions in investigative techniques which hopefully would help me track down some of those folks who were not the most law abiding of citizens. This welcomed information included the means and methods of how to treat the public I was serving, and what to look for in building a case or eventually chasing down a suspected violator. Verne Walker said, "Always treat the people you meet with the utmost respect and honesty, even those that you are charging with an offense or two," he suggested. "If you do that, I guarantee you that eventually you'll get that same respect back," he quipped.

Having had the opportunity to patrol with Verne prior to my hiring, I got to witness his ideology in action. It seemed as though everyone Verne met was proud to stand alongside of him, as they carried on a cordial and friendly conversation. That friendly hospitality even included chatting and joking with some of the worst poachers Verne had dealt with in the district he patrolled. As I headed north for my new career, I was recalling his many words of wisdom. "You're going into an area where deer poaching is a way of life for some of these folks, John. For some of them it's a business," he wisely stated. "You want to remember that not all of these people really like game wardens, as evidenced by the incident when they shot the windows out of the state-owned warden's camp late one night. And to think they did this with the warden's wife and daughter huddled together on the camp's floor, believing they were about to die," he disgustedly sputtered. "These thugs were sending a message of intimidation to the warden and to the department. I'm sure that eventually they'll try testing you too! So watch your back and stay alert," he wisely advised. "You have to remember John, it's not you personally that they despise. It's the badge you wear and the profession you are in," he said. "You are a threat to their existence as organized poachers, so I'm sure they'll be watching you closely!" he sputtered. "If and when you run across them, treat them as though they really were your friend. Don't go after them with a chip on your shoulder," he warned. "Because if you do, someone will be there who will knock that chip off of your shoulder, and they'll make the rest of your career miserable," he wisely stated. Verne's advice was priceless. His welcomed words of wisdom certainly helped establish my own personal attitude as I began this new adventure.

Then there was retired Warden Milton Scribner – still reeling from the deceitful way Jimbo, a local trapper, had hoodwinked me those first few days of my employment after I'd caught him walking out of the woods with a trap in his hand before the trapping season was to officially start – he also offered some great advice. To Scrib, for anyone to have blatantly pulled-the-wool over the eyes of one of the wardens as Jimbo had done, it was a slap-in-the-face to all of the wardens. Scrib referred to Jimbo as nothing more than a "damned snake in the grass." For years Jimbo openly bragged about his ability to avoid the law as he freely went about his many inappropriate escapades of hunting, fishing, and trapping. Now for Jimbo to be openly bragging to his buddies about this latest shady deal with the new game warden in the area, irked Scrib to no end. "You should have followed his tracks right back to where he was coming from," Scrib disgustedly stated. "I'll bet you anything that he had his equipment and bait, probably a freshly-killed dead chicken, right where he was about ready to place that trap!" he sputtered. "You had him John boy! And you had him dead to rights!" he stated. "He'd have one hell of a hard time explaining why there was a freshly-killed chicken and all of his setup gear laying right by that old log where supposedly he left his trap last year!" Scrib chuckled. "Follow the tracks. Look for signs of where people have been and where they are going, especially with any frequency," he wisely advised. "Be curious enough to follow those tracks, you'll be surprised at what you'll find," he suggested. "There's always a reason why a person heads off from the beaten trail. More often than not, you'll at least satisfy your own curiosity of what they are up to," he said.

Scrib's wise advice, along with my self-imposed ego bruising by Jimbo as he rather creatively made a fool out of this rookie warden, fired up my desire to seek out trappers within my district. In essence, I was learning more every day about their individual tactics. I tried determining how they happen to pick a certain location to place a trap, right on through their specialized techniques of being as stealth as possible, in going into and from an area where they were trapping. Follow the tracks, was great advice. There always was a sign of their presence left behind, no matter how skilled they were at trying to disguise the effort, the trail was there. I constantly found myself scanning the woods, looking for signs of where someone had traveled off of the trail.

Obviously, it was so much easier once a light layer of snow covered the area. Sometimes these tracks would head out into the woods for a short distance, where rather humorously I'd find a brown stain in the snow or a yellow spot, indicating that someone had to make an emergency bathroom run. But then, there were those times when following the tracks indicated there was something more important going on. My curiosity always took precedence in my actions, wondering where they had gone? What they were doing? And why they had chosen to go where they were going?

A perfect example was out on a back road in the town of Knox, shortly after the area had been blanketed by a light layer of fluffy snow. While on routine patrol, I noticed it appeared a vehicle had pulled off to the side of the road in a small clearing. There were telltale signs in the snow indicating where a couple of people were carrying some large item that they kept setting down in the snow, as they hiked out through a small patch of woods. Following the tracks for a short distance, I came to an area where there was a large pile of brush obviously hiding something. Whatever these folks had carried out into the woods hadn't been there for all that long, as the snow they had wallowed through was only a day or so old. Underneath the brush, I located a large outboard boat motor. Obviously, this motor was not in a normal place where one might be storing their boat motor for the winter. Upon retrieving the serial numbers from the engine and after doing a little investigative work, it was determined the boat motor had been stolen from a nearby summer residence. Retrieving stolen property, not being in the bailiwick of my official duties, I contacted one of my state police buddies, and together we worked on the case as best we could. Before day's end we were able to notify the owner of the stolen outboard motor regarding the theft, long before he even realized the motor was missing.

While retrieving the motor from the woods, I noticed a pickup truck toting a couple of young men noted for their occasional crime sprees, cruising past the area. They went by more than once. If I were to guess, I'd say they might have known what we were doing. But without the necessary proof to make a conviction, there was little we could do. The theft went unsolved. At least the owner of the stolen motor was extremely happy to get his motor back.

None of this ever would have happened, had I not heeded that wise advice from Scrib, "Follow the tracks. You never know where they will take you and why they are there!" he wisely stated. Following the tracks, listening to informants and following up on their information while treating them with respect and honesty, by far was some of the best advice this rookie warden had been given thus far. And to think it came from two of Maine's best!

Following the tracks was really quite interesting, especially when I found myself working those trappers who were suspected of not abiding by the rules of the game. My career was passing by quite quickly, leaving me wondering where to heck the time had gone? But time-wise, there was one thing about a game warden's career that most people never realized. While most folks worked a standard 40-hour work week, the wardens of my era, 1970 through the mid-1980s, never really knew how many hours we'd be working. One thing we did know, a 40-hour work week was a slow week. Our profession consisted of a non-standard work week. Often we found ourselves working for what most normal people would have considered as unacceptable hours. All of this extra work was done without overtime. We didn't get any, we didn't ask for it, nor did we expect it. Working a 100-hour week was quite common during the busy hunting season, especially when you consider the fact that it was our responsibility to cover all of the complaints within our districts 24 hours a day.

On top of that, the nighttime required many hours of surveillance trying to capture those hunters who were intent on shooting a deer underneath a bright light. These night hunting efforts alone, required many extra hours in the field, patiently watching and waiting if we were to curtail the activity. It was our jobs to cover our assigned districts, when and if the needs demanded. Seldom was there not a need! We made up for the extra time we worked during the course of the busy hunting season at a later time when things were much quieter and we had the freedom to take the time off that we wanted. That freedom of choice was a benefit in itself. For most of us, we knew the requirements of a warden's job when we signed up for duty. We loved what we were doing and we enjoyed the freedoms we'd been given to perform our jobs.

For me personally, I never considered my duties as work. I was *living the dream* and who could ask for anything more? So it was in October of 1979 when I found myself checking an area in the town of Knox, searching for more signs of illegal trapping activity. Once again, this information came as the result of another disgruntled trapper who wanted to "let me in on a little secret!"

Like the previous seasons, another trapper was reportedly making an early start on the trapping season. Supposedly this individual was trapping for fisher, fox, and raccoon. And like so many of those trappers before him, he was not checking his traps every 24 hours, not labeling them with his name and address as required by law, and he was trapping on land where he knew he wasn't welcomed. All of these violations were inclusive of the trapping during closed season violation, should he be apprehended.

My informant was quick to remind me that I had captured this man's brother, Dwight, a few years earlier. Now it appears the two brothers were both reverting back to their own set of rules and that they were in need of a little more attention in the enforcement efforts. The informant said, "scan the area for motorbike tracks out on the remote backwoods roads and along the edges of recently-harvested corn fields. If you see these bike tracks, you're definitely in the right area!" he advised. "Just look for places where they appear to have stopped and follow the tracks!" he repeated. I'd certainly heard that message before! The informant stated how the two brothers usually left home early in the morning hours, heading in different directions. Their illegal trapping territory had been expanded to several surrounding towns. Especially now that they had a better means of traveling into these rural places. Their illegal activities had definitely infuriated many of those honest trappers within the area. People who were reputable and who suddenly found their own trapping domains being invaded by these two poachers – poachers who were operating on their own greedy agendas and to hell with anyone who might get in their way. It was time to start cruising the woods roads and cornfields, searching for any signs of motorbike tracks and placing some extra time into investigating this illegal trapping activity.

I decided to begin my search close to where Dwight's brother, Roy, lived. Roy's home was surrounded by several large cornfields, places where the area farmers were raising silage corn for their cattle. These fields had already been harvested, so it should be fairly easy to find the bike tracks, if in fact he was leaving from his house. Hiding my cruiser, I struck out on foot, planning to spend the day going wherever the trail might lead me.

It was a real foggy morning. The misty cover was perfect, as I slowly went around Roy's house and into the nearby cornfield. The fog was so thick I barely could see more than twenty feet in front of me. Sure enough, I found the motorbike tracks skirting along the edge of the fields. Some of these tracks appeared to be extremely fresh, but it was hard to tell. As I slowly hiked along, suddenly a short distance in front of me I observed the motorbike parked along the edge of the woods. "Surely I can't be this lucky," I thought.

It was a rare occasion when we wardens had luck like this happening to us. I ducked into the bushes along the edge of the field, observing the area, while waiting for Roy to return to his machine. I could hear him floundering around in the woods a short distance away. It sounded as though he was standing in one spot, pounding on something. Something like maybe setting a #220 Conibear trap to a tree! It wasn't long before Roy exited the area, climbed aboard the small motorbike and was headed my way. I quickly stepped in front of him, motioning for him to stop. The look on his face was one of total shock and disbelief. "Hi John," he said, "What the hell are you doing way out here so early in the morning?"

"I was about to ask you the same thing!" I said, as I noted a small basket filled with trapping equipment attached to the front of his bike, confirming the fact that he indeed was trapping. There was a bag containing a few dead chickens strapped alongside of the bike. I also noticed Roy was toting a holstered weapon on his side.

"Is that weapon you're toting there loaded, Roy," I inquired.

"It is," he rather sheepishly replied.

"Do you have a concealed weapon permit, allowing you to carry it loaded?" I calmly inquired.

"No, I don't," he humbly sputtered.

"Well Roy, I'm sure you know that legally you can't carry a loaded weapon on a motor vehicle," I informed him. "And what about these traps you are setting Roy? Are they properly marked with your name and address on them, even though the season has yet to open?" I asked.

"I think so! I might have forgotten to label some, but I don't think I did!" he nervously responded.

"Well Roy, the reason I'm asking is because recently I've seized several unlabeled traps scattered around the area. Illegally set traps with no names, and most all of them left unattended," I stated. "My information is pretty reliable Roy, that these illegal sets belong to you and your brother Dwight. I'd strongly suggest that maybe you guys might want to start abiding by the rules." I stressed. "Now, how about that trap you just placed down in the woods there Roy, is it properly labeled?" I calmly inquired. Truth be known, I wasn't really sure if he had placed a trap down in the woods or not. But the odds were pretty good that he had, even though I hadn't gone in to find it yet! There was no other reason to explain his purpose for being down there in the thick woods.

"I'm not sure if it is or not," he humbly stated. I could tell just from his response and actions, that it wasn't! Together we hiked down into the area to where Roy had placed a #220 Conibear trap on a slanted tree. I took possession of the trap for evidence, as I passed Roy a couple of summonses, along with a stern warning that he and Dwight might want to be retracing their tracks and picking up any more of the traps they had out. I advised him that they needed to pay close attention to the rules, that I would be searching several areas on tips that I had recently received and if I found any more illegal sets I'd be back with more court summonses. I made it perfectly clear I'd be watching from afar, seizing any traps I found that were not legally set.

We actually parted company that morning on a fairly friendly note, all things considered. Roy reassured me he would remedy the situation. With a halfhearted promise he stated he'd take care of it. I took him at his word! A week later, I received another message from yet another trapper inquiring, "Do you want to capture Roy for trapping illegally?" he sputtered.

I quickly explained, "I just did last week. Do you have something new to offer?" I rather inquisitively asked.

"I sure do," he snickered. "And it's a good piece of information," he exclaimed. "I know exactly where you can find another one of his illegally set traps. It's placed in an area far away from his home and far away from where you caught him the last time," the informant stated. "This trap has no tag on it, but I know how you can prove it's his!" he boldly chirped.

"How do you propose I'm going to be able to prove it?" I quizzed the informant.

"Well John, if you go up to where this trap is placed, laying right near the illegal trap, is his wallet," he snickered. "All of his identification and a decent amount of money is included," he loudly chuckled. "I didn't remove it from where it lay, but I'll be glad to show you exactly where it is and you can take it from there!" he advised. "Ain't no way he can deny this trap as not being his," he snickered.

Out of curiosity I asked, "Are there any motorbike tracks near the area?"

"As I recall, there were!" the informant stated. "Damn it all John, most of us try to abide by the rules and these guys just don't seem to care! It's not fair. They always seem to have a habit of trapping by their own set of rules and to hell with the rest of us, who try to remain legal," the informant griped. "I know you're trying to do your very best, but you need our help! I'm willing to gladly give you whatever help I can," he offered.

Shortly after that phone conversation, we met. Following the informant, we proceeded to hike up to Pond Hill in the town of Brooks. Sure enough, the motorbike tracks were obvious in the loose gravel along the woods road leading up to the area. The informant led me out into the woods to where the sprung trap was resting. Sure enough, laying on the ground nearby, was Roy's wallet. The scene was just as the informant had described. Roy's identification was included, along with a decent amount of cash. Once again, this was way too easy! Roy could be thankful this trapper was as honest as the day was long. Maybe in the long run, Roy and his brother Dwight, could learn something from this man's honesty.

Gathering up the evidence, the next day I arrived at Roy's house. "What the hell do you want now?" he disgustedly sputtered. "Damn it, I took your advice and cleaned up my act," he reassured me.

I calmly said, "Roy, I've got some good news for you and then I have some bad. Which would you prefer to get first?" I smirked.

"Well I can't imagine anything being too bad, so what's the good news?" he asked.

"Did you happen to have lost your wallet somewhere?" I inquired.

I noticed a look of sheer relief appear on his face as he said, "I did, but I don't have a clue where. I lost it a day or two ago," he quipped. "All of my licenses and stuff are in it. Do you happen to have it I hope?" he rather pathetically begged.

"I do Roy, I have it right here," I responded. "Do you have any idea how much money you might have had in it at the time?" I inquired.

"Oh, I'm thinking maybe $70 to $80," he replied. "Well apparently someone was being good to you, there's $120 in it," I said, as I quickly handed the wallet over to him.

"Damn, am I ever some relieved to get that back," he excitedly sputtered. "Now, what supposedly is all of this bad news you seem to have?" he asked.

"Well Roy, it seems you lost your wallet up on Pond Hill in Brooks, right alongside another one of those illegal traps you'd set," I explained. "So now Roy, I have another summons for you, similar to the ones I gave you a few days ago!" I calmly informed him. "I told you I'd be watching from afar!" I quipped. "Apparently you didn't take me seriously!" I boldly stated. "I'm serious about this illegal activity Roy and I hope this time you'll take me more seriously. I'd hate to have to come back yet again!" I barked, again trying to emphasize my point.

"I hear ya John, I hear ya!" he yelled, as he humbly seized the summons from my hand. "Can I take care of this one through the mail like I did the last time?" he asked.

"Not now Roy. The court won't let you take care of it without an appearance before the judge. Especially for a second violation in such a short period of time," I stated. "I'm sure the judge is going to want to speak to you directly. Maybe he can finally get the point across to you guys much better than I'm doing," I responded.

"I assure you John, I've got the *@# damned message. I'm pulling all of the traps I have tomorrow and to hell with this trapping business," he disgustedly shouted. "I've had enough of this bull---- for one season," he muttered.

I replied, "Maybe you can speak to your brother Dwight and wisely advise him of the same thing!" I said, as I turned and walked away. "I'm hearing he still has a few illegal sets out and I'm on the prowl!" I stated as I was returning to my cruiser ready to depart Roy's driveway.

As luck had it, a few days later I managed to apprehend Roy's brother Dwight once again. Apparently, if Roy had given

Dwight the message, like so many times before, Dwight simply ignored it and continued doing as he damn well pleased. Dwight was using a motorbike, similar to Roy's. One equipped with a little box on the front to carry his gear and a bag attached with dead chickens to be used for bait. Once again, lady luck was on my side. I was watching an area where I suspected Dwight had pre-baited with chickens much earlier in the summer. I knew it was just a matter of time before he'd return to set his traps, once the fall weather arrived and the pelts were in their prime. This area was on a remote dirt road that lead into some gravel pits in the town of Thorndike. I decided to dedicate a little time to periodically watching the area, hoping that he'd been back to set his traps. Once I knew they had been placed there, I'd work it hard.

Upon my arrival, I hid my cruiser and walked a short distance, checking to see if the traps had been set. The dead chicken was still in its place, obviously having been discovered by predators as it was pretty well chewed up and mangled. I was just turning to leave, when off in the distance I heard the puttering of a motor bike that seemed to be heading my way. The timing couldn't have been any better! I ran up on top of the gravel bank, sliding underneath a few bushes in order to conceal myself. It was a perfect location to observe the area.

Sure enough, Dwight came puttering into the area as carefree as a bird, never expecting the warden would be watching his every move. Dwight exited the bike, walked around the front, grabbed his ax and a #220 Conibear trap. He then quickly headed into the woods, where the old dead chicken had been hanging from its marker. I slithered out from under the bushes and started his way, so as to confront him directly when he emerged from the woods. I was almost there when he suddenly reappeared. Glancing my way, he started running for his motorbike, as I was high-tailing it toward him, screaming for him to stop. But he quickly got the little machine started, shooting on past me like he had been shot out of a gun! I was yelling for him to stop but he ignored the requests, almost striking me as he scooted on past, heading down the narrow dirt road and away from the area just as fast as the little motorbike would go. It didn't really matter. I knew where he lived and I certainly knew who he was. I went down into the woods, retrieving the unlabeled trap that he had just set, seizing it for evidence. I then headed for Dwight's house, where once again lady luck was on my side. I arrived there just as he was pulling into the driveway. I slid in right behind him. The greeting I received was anything but cordial! He demanded that I get the *#*! off his property, making it very clear that he wasn't about to take any *&%@ damned summons. Nor would he be making any court appearance, if I thought that was what I was coming there for.

I calmly wrote out the summonses for the violations, dropping it at his feet with the stern warning that if he should decide to ignore the legal court order, I'd gladly return with an arrest warrant, providing him with an all-expense paid trip to the Waldo County Crowbar Hotel, otherwise known as the Waldo County Jail! One way or another, he'd be making his appearance before the District Court Judge. The choice was his, however he wanted to do it. I managed to say, "If you fail to show up on the assigned date, I guarantee you the consequences will be far worse than what you're facing right now, Dwight! So once again, the choice is yours!" I sputtered, as I climbed back into my cruiser and left. I could have arrested him right on the spot, for failing to stop for an officer and for the trapping violation, but I was quite sure he was subtly starting to get the message that this trapping illegally wasn't a guarantee that he had free rein to do as he damn well pleased. And to think, Dwight had been the one who had turned Curly in for his illegal trapping activities a time before, calling him the thief of all thieves!

Through it all, I quickly realized that obviously there is no love or loyalty between some of these poachers. These few men proved that point quite well! Just for the record, Dwight made a wise move by appearing in court on the day he was supposed to. Upon hearing the facts of the case, and after viewing Dwight's previous record, the judge lowered the boom on him. He was assessed a hefty fine and had his license to trap suspended for a lengthy period of time – not that I figured a license suspension would ever stop him should he decide to continue doing what he had been. These two trappers, who so routinely ignored the rules of the game, never realized that their sins had been reported by their own fellow trappers. Honest folks who were protecting their own interest and the hobby they enjoyed. Thank God, I listened to Milt Scribner and Verne Walker and followed the tracks after receiving the information of those who put me onto the right trail.

Who is this Mystery Trapper?

During the winter of 1982 I found myself involved in an unusual closed season trapping investigation. The state had been blanketed with a fair amount of snow in February during what had been a long winter season. Normally this is what I considered as a quiet time of the year for warden work within my patrol area. Other than checking a few beaver trappers on the beaver ponds scattered around the district, or patrolling the many miles of snowmobile trails that skirted throughout the area, there was not too much to do. The many miles of snowmobile trails were well organized and marked trails that the various newly created snowmobile clubs had established. Snowmobiling across the state was still kind of in its infancy. But it was rapidly becoming a winter time activity that was gaining in popularity all over our state.

As these machines grew in popularity, the Maine State Legislature willed the law enforcement powers to the warden service. This was yet another task forced upon the agency by the powers that be, but it was a great way for us wardens to spend a cold winter day in the great out-of-doors during a time when patrolling was somewhat boring. The well-groomed and maintained snowmobile trails ran through the deep woods from one end of our state to the other. The machines themselves were becoming much more dependable and capable of reaching speeds that prior to then would have been totally unimaginable. I could easily unload my sled in one town and spend the entire day cruising through the backcountry into areas where I'd never been before.

Deputy Warden Scott Sienkiewicz was great company, as he tagged along on his own sled, while we scoured the many deer yards, checking for signs of predators that might be threatening the herd. We spent hours out in the backcountry looking for signs of illegal activity that we might possibly want ourselves getting involved in. Especially in those areas where it appeared someone may have been up to no good, or some areas where certain folks never expected the eyes of the law to be visiting. A perfect example of finding the unexpected while on a daytime excursion came one day in January, 1975, when we were traveling through the woods along one of these snowmobile trails.

As we rounded the bend we observed a young fellow with a shotgun standing alongside the well-groomed trail. I was wearing my state-issued snowmobile suit, which at the time gave no indication that I was a game warden. There were no patches, badges, or other identifying marks, indicating my official capacity. Pulling up alongside the young man without identifying myself, I simply inquired, "Hi there! Whatcha hunting for way to heck out here and at this time of the year?"

The young man politely stated, "Rabbits! My dog is running them all around this place, and so far I've had great luck," as he held up three of the snow hares he had bagged.

"Oh wow!" I said, "That looks like fun!" I chuckled. "Do you have a hunting license to do this?" I politely asked.

"Hell no!" he responded. "I doubt you'll ever see a game warden way to heck out here?" he wisely smirked.

I immediately shut my snow sled off, and in a move that must have looked like Superman changing into his flying suit inside of a telephone booth, I quickly unzipped my snowmobile suit, exposing the uniform I was wearing underneath it. "Well I hate to ruin your day, but guess what?" I half-heartedly smirked. "You don't have to doubt no more. Today you're seeing a game warden way to heck out here!" I sputtered.

That sick look, almost like a kid caught with his hand in the cookie jar after his mom forbade him to have any cookies, was quite obvious on the young man's face.

"You're kidding me!" he mumbled, as he humbly accepted the court summons I was writing out. I'm sure that on this particular day, he never in his wildest dreams expected to have a game warden come cruising through the area where he was hunting. Especially being so far away from everything.

Slowly cruising over these snowmobile trails was a rewarding way to spend a cool wintery day. It was a special treat to be passing a small herd of deer watching our every move, as we slowly maneuvered through one of their deer yards. We actually were helping them by packing down the deep snow trails making their traveling so much easier. It was quite enjoyable, occasionally witnessing a fox jumping into the trail ahead of us as we slowly cruised through that portion of deep woods that the fox considered its home. But that's not the story I intended to tell.

On one of our random excursions in late February of 1982, as we traveled along the trails in the backcountry, between the towns of Knox and Freedom, I noticed where someone had wandered out through the deep snow and away from the snowmobile trail. Their path was an old one, with snow filling in the footprints. But it appeared as though this was not the customary short bathroom excursion one might have expected after a long ride. Recalling those sacred words of my mentors to "follow the tracks," I thought I might as well investigate to see just where these tracks will take me and why they went there? But nonetheless curiosity got the best of me. I just had to see where they would lead. Thinking of Retired Warden Milton Scribner drilling into my head, "follow the tracks, you just might be surprised at what you find!" I seized upon the moment, as I wallowed out through the path following the barely visible trail left in the deep snow. I fully expected to go a short distance, only to find a spot in the snow where someone had made an emergency bathroom run. But these tracks seemed to be heading farther and farther away from the snowmobile trail. Much farther than I would have expected for anyone to have been making a bathroom run. Off in the distance, I noticed a partially fallen down tree that didn't seem to look quite right. Upon reaching the area, I found where someone had carefully placed hemlock branches concealing what was on the other side of the partially fallen tree. I said to Scott, "I bet someone has a fisher set on that

A view of the illegal fisher set looking up the fallen down tree.
Rabbit was the bait!

tree. They either left the boughs there after the season officially ended months ago, or they are illegally trapping fisher right now in the dead of winter."

Sure enough, halfway up the fallen tree was a #220 Conibear trap, carefully concealed in the fir boughs. Nailed securely to the upper side of the tree was a dead rabbit, used to draw the animals into the site. I was amazed that anyone would be attempting to trap fisher this time of the year, especially so long after the season had officially ended and during a time when their pelts wouldn't be in as good a shape as if they were trapped late in the fall. I began wondering if there were more of these sets to be found. More so, I wondered who this mystery trapper could possibly be? Whoever this was, made sure that from their viewpoint while cruising along the snowmobile trail they could see if anything was in the traps simply by observing the area from the trail itself. The real task at hand would be trying to find out just who this person was. Who could be trapping fisher illegally in the dead of winter and again was this the only set they have out here in the countryside?

After photographing the scene and removing the boughs, we seized the unlabeled trap for evidence. Evidence that would be needed to get a prosecution, if we were fortunate enough to find out who this mysterious trapper might be? To explain the workings of these traps, a fisher scenting the dead rabbit and in search of an easy meal, would scamper up the tree heading for the bait – bait strategically placed upon the upper side of the bough-covered trap. As the fisher ducks through the boughs and directly through the square jaws of the trap, the metal shaped V prongs that you see hanging down from the top of the trap in the accompanying photo is the trigger.

The photo above shows the #220 Conibear trap. No one would ever be the wiser that there were traps set nearby, other than the culprit who had set them.

Once the fisher brushes against the trigger, it releases the powerful jaws of the trap, instantly killing the animal by breaking its neck. Cruel as it sounds, it is a very quick and instantaneous death. After accidentally stumbling upon this illegal set, Scott and I decided if there was one, there must be more just like it scattered along the well-traveled snowmobile trails. Over the next few days we scoured the area cruising all of the trails we could fine. We were searching for any signs of where someone had hiked off the beaten path.

It wasn't long before we found another place where someone had once again hiked out into the woods. Just like before, the old tracks left in the snow brought us to yet another dead tree that had fallen halfway to the ground. Placed upon this tree was another group of boughs, obviously concealing yet another trap. This one however had a rather unique and different bait. It was a far different setup than anything I'd ever seen before, nor anything I've seen since.

Secured to the tree a short distance above the trap was a large fish head, that of a lake trout that someone had recently caught. Nailed securely to the tree and just below the fish head was the carcass of a domestic house cat. Whoever this mystery trapper was, it appeared he was using whatever means of bait he happened to stumble across. I could only imagine what would have happened had those nationally protesting organizations, who so vehemently despised trapping, happened across a scene such as this. For them to illustrate a house cat being used as fisher bait, would generate a lot of hate and support for their cause, from every cat owner in the country. Whoever this culprit was could single handedly ruin the reputations of many of those legal trappers who year after year abided by the rules of the game. That one bad apple syndrome needed to be harvested and held responsible for his sins. The sooner the better!

Scott and I needed to stay on top of this, hopefully bringing an end to the illegal trapping activity. But where to start? Most people engaging in this type of an illegal activity could care less about the rules of the game or the damage they could do to the

This illegal trapper was using fish heads and even a domestic cat for fisher bait.

sport itself if they were left unchecked. Obviously, the high prices for a fisher pelt and the greed to cash in on the golden opportunity, overrode any sense of decency to some people. This trapper apparently was one of them! I often wondered how this illegal trapper came into possession of that house cat. I hope it wasn't someone's pet that had been purposely slaughtered simply to attract a fisher. But then again, I reckon if this person was so blatantly willing to disregard the fish and game laws, more than likely he wasn't afraid to violate those rules of society. Rules such as the cruelty to animals statutes. Their thinking probably being, "Who would ever miss a damned old cat!" I could only imagine the horror that could come from a picture like this during the next trapping season. Especially from the anti-trappers who already were raising havoc all across the nation in their well-planned attempts to get the sport banned.

Over the next few days we canvassed the area the best we could, constantly digging out more traps, some of them ground sets, where this individual possibly could catch a variety of other wildlife species. With each new find, we noticed how well concealed these sets had been placed. And yet they all were within sight of the snowmobile trail. Whoever placed them some time before the snow started piling up, didn't have to leave tracks in the snow to check them. All they had to do was simply cruise past on their snowmobile while closely observing the area where the trap was left.

As we continued hunting for more illegal sets, spending hours scouring the sides of the narrow trails for any signs of human activity, we found several more. In one of those excursions as we hiked through the woods following the old tracks left in the snow, I glanced ahead to see a dead fisher hanging from the tree. This time the illegal trapper had been successful in his efforts, but unsuccessful in getting his paws on the cache'. Seizing the illegally set trap and the large male fisher, after photographing the scene and gathering any evidence we could find, we still were no closer in determining who this person could be. Like the other illegal sets, this one had been baited with a dead snowshoe hare, and another large lake trout head. Whoever the culprit was, obviously had been quite

successful on his ice fishing excursions. Certainly whoever it was, wasn't catching those big fish anywhere near our area. The patrol district I had was not noted for its great ice fishing, especially for lake trout the size of these monsters. Without much other information to go on, it appeared as though the only chances of ever apprehending this mysterious illegal trapper, was hopefully from someone out in the community to come forward with a little helpful information. Information that possibly would help steer us in the right direction of solving just who this mystery trapper could be. I doubted I'd hear from the trappers themselves, as the season had ended long ago and I was sure they were not thinking about their trade and, even more so, who would be trapping in mid-winter, especially so long after the legal trapping season had ended.

The only chance I had, was to place my trust in a few of the confidential informants who had helped me so much in the past, hoping maybe that they might hear or see something that would help us out. Most of these trappers were busily negotiating with the fur buyers trying to get the best price possible for their hard work. The few people I entrusted with my information, were absolutely shocked and upset that someone would be so brazen as to be trapping in the dead of winter. After all, it was their sport and their future that this person was abusing. The fisher's pelt taken at this time of the year would be far from prime. It would be almost worthless to any sharp-eyed fur buyer. The other problem being, that whoever this person was, couldn't sell his pelts until a warden had inspected the hide and snapped the necessary non-removal tag upon it, approving it as being legally harvested. At this time of the year we wardens didn't even have the tags to do so if we had to. All of those items had been turned into the biologists for establishing harvest numbers and deciding the future dates for the next season. More than likely, whoever the culprit was, he'd simply have to store the pelt until next year's season before bringing them to a warden for inspection. On one of our day-long trap hunting excursions I took my young son, John Jr., along with me. He thoroughly loved riding on the snow machine and participating in the hunt. The picture on the right came from one of our daily finds, as he carried the snowshoe hare back to my machine.

I spent many evenings reviewing the trapping records, seeking people who may have been trapping within the same area where we were finding these sets. I acquired a half dozen names of trappers that I personally knew very well from the area. None of them seemed to be the type of individual I'd expect to be so blatantly violating the rules. But then again, I never was surprised by what I might find. Occasionally those I trusted the most, had a few skeletons in the closet. But they were few and far between. For now the investigation had come to a complete standstill. I'd run out of places to look and suspects to find. In general conversation at a local coffee shop where several of us often congregated, over a light lunch and a cup of hot coffee, I casually inquired from the crew around the table if any of them had heard about someone from the area catching

Little John, as I called him, managed to get in on the action.
A great day with dad out on the trails

some large lake trout. I was hoping someone might know of a local individual who was bragging about the large fish they were catching elsewhere. After all, fishermen certainly do like telling their fish stories. I thought, if nothing else, this might give me a name of the person who was using these fish heads for fisher bait. I didn't let on the real reasons for my inquiry! I didn't want the public knowing this illegal activity was occurring in their backyards, especially disclosing the fact that someone in the crowd just might have been missing their pet cat – a cat brutally taken for the purpose of enticing a fisher to meet its own demise. Like so often happens with any investigation, the investigator needs a bit of luck. Hopefully, that luck would come before we had to totally give up on the effort.

Two weeks later, I received a phone call from one of my confidential informants. "John, have you had any luck on solving that illegal trapping case?" he inquired.

"Nothing yet," I humbly stated.

"Well I might have a little something for you," he stated. "It seems as though there's a fellow over in that area where you found them traps, that has been going to some lake down in

Hancock County ice fishing," he said. "I'm told he has been catching some monster lake trout down there. He's been bragging to a few of my friends about his good luck!" he continued. "Now, I'm not saying he's your man, but I do know he is a trapper and he does have an old snowmobile that he keeps out behind his house. His house connects right to the trails where you fellas been finding them traps," he advised.

I could feel the adrenaline rush flowing into my veins, as I carefully listened to every word my friend was stating. The circumstances were a long way from proving anything, but at least we had a name and a place to start looking again. The next day, with my trusty Deputy, Scott Sienkiewicz, seated alongside, we went to where this individual lived. The house was exactly where the informant stated, right in the middle of the trails where we'd been finding these traps. Without anything more to go on, I decided to confront the landowner directly, hoping to get a confession of sorts. The chances were slim, but the chances of us getting to this point in the investigation had been even slimmer.

As we drove into the yard, the garage door was open, exposing several #220 Conibear traps and a few leg-hold traps hanging from the wall. Located nearby was a large chest freezer. I couldn't help but wonder what was inside the freezer, but without a warrant, and a whole lot more information than what I had, I wasn't legally about to find out.

Parked alongside the garage was an Arctic Cat snowmobile, and a trail that went through their backyard and out onto the main trail where we found most of these illegal traps. As we stepped outside of the vehicle, the door opened and a woman met us in the driveway. "Can I help you?" she inquired, as she curiously looked us up and down, obviously wondering why we were there. I calmly explained we were game wardens and inquired, "Is your husband by any chance home? I would like to speak to him if possible," I politely stated.

"No, he has gone fishing until tomorrow. Is there anything wrong?' she asked.

"Oh no, nothing serious," I replied, "I'd heard he was catching some nice fish through the ice and I knew it wasn't around here, I'm just curious as to where he has been going. I might want to head that way myself one day!" I kind of fibbed, hoping to put her at ease.

"Oh, he's had a great winter ice fishing. That's where he and a buddy are right now," she volunteered. "I'd tell you where but I honestly can't recall the name of the lake. Somewhere in the Ellsworth area," she boasted. "He should be back tomorrow afternoon if you wish to speak with him!" she offered.

I said, "That's great, I'll try to swing back tomorrow afternoon or early evening if it's okay with you folks."

"He should be back by then," she calmly replied. "I'll tell him you were here."

I wanted her to keep our little visit a secret, but I knew I couldn't. I didn't want to alert her as to the real reason why we were there. As I left, I couldn't help but notice the string of traps hanging from inside the garage wall. There were both Conibear and leg-holds – the same types of traps that we had been seizing. I had a gut feeling we were at the right place, but proving it would be a little more difficult.

The next afternoon, Scott and I returned to Dan's home. The pickup truck was in the yard when we arrived, indicating that Dan had returned from his fishing trip. As we walked into the garage to knock on the door, I noticed the string of traps that were hanging on the wall yesterday were no longer visible. It appeared as though Dan might have suspected our real reasons for the earlier visit. He had obviously removed any possible signs of evidence that could implicate him as being the mystery trapper. After a few minutes of interrogating Dan, there was no doubt in my mind that he was the culprit we were seeking. He was very humble and non-committal to the questions we asked. This case was very circumstantial at best, but I left Dan with a couple of summonses on that day, satisfied in my own mind that we had solved the mystery.

Dan never bothered arguing his innocence, nor did he protest the summonses to the degree an innocent person would be expected to react. Unlike most people who when handed a summons, they quite boisterously claim they are innocent of any charges levied against them. Instead Dan was kind of laid back and reserved. He refused to allow a consent search of the chest freezer in the garage which was located close to where the string of traps had been the day before – a chest freezer that possibly could have had a few fisher pelts captured from earlier times. But without legal authorization to take a peek, I never would know what the freezer contained. When confronted about the missing string of traps hanging from his garage walls the day before, Dan simply stated, "Oh I decided to take them into my cellar, to prepare them for future use during next year's trapping season!"

In the end Dan paid an attorney to represent his day in court. Because it was such a circumstantial case, the attorney and the county prosecutor mutually agreed to a mild plea bargain deal. Dan agreed to plead guilty to the trapping out of season charge if the other charges were dismissed. The county prosecutor thought the offer was a fair deal under the given conditions, as he readily accepted the attorney's offer. Dan was assessed a $50 fine for his illegal activity and the matter was legally resolved.

Although it seemed as though justice was weak in this matter, it at least brought about a conviction. If Dan had just one fisher in that chest freezer, he still was far ahead of the game, especially realizing that a decent fisher pelt was worth upwards to $300. The only justice we got for all the effort and time we put into chasing this mysterious trapper down, was knowing that Dan's trapping license was suspended for a 2-year period. But then again, what difference did it make? He was trapping in closed season to begin with, which meant there was no license to cover his illegal activity in the first place. Possibly if he decided to trap again he simply would be more cautious.

Once again, justice works in a mysterious way, but it's still the best system in the world! Or so they say! I wasn't completely thrilled with the prosecutor and the judge's penalties in the matter. Especially considering all the hours and time invested into bringing the case forward. But then who was I to say? Scott and I had done our jobs by bringing the case to the court for a resolution. From that point forward the matter was entirely out of our hands. Hopefully Dan learned a valuable lesson. If not, I was sure our paths would more than likely cross again!

Helping the Needy, Building Trust, and Gathering Informants

Over a period of time, and as I became better acquainted with the folks living within my district, I realized who I could trust and who I couldn't. Likewise, they too learned whether they could trust me. I also became acquainted with several families who desperately were struggling to make ends meet, mostly large farming families with incomes barely supporting their needs. The many welfare programs that are so readily available in today's times were unheard of back then. It made perfect sense for us wardens to provide them with an occasional deer or some other form of game that needed to be disposed of which could be properly used by those individuals in need. Such as salvageable deer from a number of road kills, or illegally seized game taken from some poacher who suddenly found himself being caught with his hands in the cookie jar.

In those days the farmers had large families. For many of them, the times were tough trying to provide a meal.

169

Occasionally they'd blister a deer underneath a light to meet that need. They never bragged about having done it, nor did they waste any of the meat. Many of the government welfare programs that are in place today were yet to be established. For a few of these folks they had truly fallen upon hard times. We wardens pretty well knew what was happening. As long as they were not openly bragging about their dastardly deeds, and as long as we were not getting complaints of their occasional activities, these people were not as actively pursued as the die-hard poacher, who was killing and slaughtering the deer for a profit and a challenge, just to see what they could get away with.

Believe it or not, there was an organized group of individuals who were actively poaching deer both day and night and then selling the meat to anyone who was willing to pay their asking price. Amazingly, the market was a thriving business to a few of these individuals. Especially during the busy hunting seasons when the nonresidents invaded the area, all of them in pursuit of a monster buck of their own. A few of those nonresidents who had been unsuccessful in their hunting efforts, desperately wanted a trophy to take back home to show off in front of their buddies in order to brag about being the great hunters that they had been. When in reality, some of them never left the hunting camp to go hunting after a week or two of constant partying with their buddies. They just had to have something to take home in order to confirm the excuse that they had been to hunting camp and put forth a great time of hunting. This is when the call would go out to the gang of poachers. For a price, their order would be filled. The bigger the buck, the higher the price!

It was indeed a booming business for the gang during the hunting season. It was these organized poachers who were the people who needed to be held accountable for their sins, not the poor farmer who occasionally shot a deer to feed his family. After all, for the most part, it was the wild animals within the area who were living off of the farmer's produce and hard work all summer long meeting their own needs, so what really was wrong with a farmer taking one every now and then, especially if it was destroying his crops. Legally it was against the law, but priority-wise, it wasn't at the top of our list of things to do. It was those organized poachers who were profiting from their efforts, or the excitement they got from pursuing a night hunting jaunt, hoping to see just what they could get away with, who I considered to be the real culprits at the top of my most wanted list.

Whenever possible, I'd seek out people within my patrol area who were in need of a little help and give them a road-killed deer or other fish and game species. These were people who could use a little extra meat to feed their families and were willing to properly dispose of a critter if it was given to them. Quite often I found myself delivering a deer carcass to some of these folks, requiring them to get out of bed in the middle of the night in order to butcher the carcass and to properly care for the meat before it spoiled. Seldom, if ever, did they gripe or complain and never was the offer refused. Every now and then these folks would return the favor by passing along a little information to help solve a major case that had been placed on the back burner for a lack of leads and evidence. But they mostly did so with the stipulation that they remain anonymous. Providing information to assist our efforts wasn't in any way a requirement for them being placed on the donor list, just to be clear.

Occasionally however, they'd provide some helpful information at a time when it seemed an open investigation was at a dead end, making it impossible to successfully solve a major crime. A prime example of such an incident happened within the very first year of my young career. I was called to investigate a hunting accident in the town of Thorndike. A deer hunter had been seriously injured, with the shooter fleeing the scene after firing three rapid shots at the victims as they sat perched along the edge of a field during the final few minutes of the legal hunting hours. The seriously-wounded hunter had been transported to a Waterville hospital with non-life-threatening injuries. Two bullets whizzed between the heads of the two hunting buddies as they were seated close together in a field, just at the edge of dark. The third shot entered the back side of the victim's right arm, blowing out his bicep. The bullet continued across his chest, leaving a groove in the fabric of his hunting jacket. That single shot came within a fraction of an inch of being fatal.

This incident happened just prior to the mandatory blaze orange hunting color law being implemented. Realizing his grave mistake, the perpetrator quickly fled the scene on foot, leaving the wounded hunter and his buddy laying precariously on the edge of the woods to fend for themselves. For the next two years Hunter Safety Officer, John Marsh, and I were constantly following up on several leads. Each time never getting any closer to finding out who the shooter had been. We had a suspect in mind – someone living nearby who quite possibly may have been the shooter, but without the required evidence to prove our case, we seemingly arrived at a dead end in resolving the incident.

Evidence was gathered at the scene and properly secured. A short distance from where the victim and his friend had been sitting along the edge of the old field among some small shrubs, three spent .300 Savage rifle cartridges were located in the area from where the shots had been fired. A short distance away, in a woods road leading out of the area, we found an old dirty green hat and a few hairs embedded in a broken tree branch, where obviously the shooter had rapidly fled the scene. The hat appeared to have been knocked off the shooter's head as he fled out through the woods, hurrying away from the area. In his haste to flee the scene he never bothered stopping to retrieve the hat! Also, there were a couple of clumps of human hair entangled in the low hanging branch, right near where the hat was located. But these hair samples, although collected, were of little use since the technical DNA procedures we are so accustomed to today were non-existent back in that time. This collected evidence was only known to those of us in law enforcement and then only to the ones who were investigating the incident.

But after several days and weeks of investigating the incident, unfortunately we were no closer to finding the responsible party. The case had come to a complete standstill, until something more promising transpired to provide us with more information to go on. Fast forward two years later, when I happened upon a young man with a large family fishing at Unity Pond. There were schools of white perch congregating along the shoreline. His young kids were scurrying about the area, leaving the dad all alone tending to the fishing poles. I watched as the dad was intently seeking a mess of the white perch in order to feed his family. These perch would make a perfect chowder. Providing yet another inexpensive meal which would help in getting the family through the financially hard times they were experiencing.

Upon approaching the young man I quickly determined he was fishing without the proper fishing license as required by law. I knew if he had to go to court to pay a fine for the misdemeanor offense and was ordered by the courts to pay a penalty, this would deprive the family of yet more hard-earned money that it desperately needed to put food on the table. I also knew the young man's family and was well aware of how hard this young man had been struggling to provide the very best he could for all of them, during a time when all of the social programs and other governmental handouts of today did not exist. In good conscience, I didn't feel right making the family suffer any more than they already were. But by the same token, I simply couldn't just walk away pretending I hadn't seen anything. The fact that the young man quickly owned up to his neglect to buy a fishing license and that he was willing to accept whatever consequences were thrown at him, was another example of his honesty and integrity. He openly admitted that his intentions were for the kids to do all of the fishing, and he'd help them as they provided the fish for him to take home.

He simply stated that, "I just didn't have the necessary funds to buy a fishing license, John." But as often happens when a bunch of youngsters lose their attention span while fishing, they had wandered away from the task of fishing and were busily engaged in chasing frogs and turtles in a nearby marsh. This left dad attending to the fishing rods and capturing a meal for his family by himself. I wrote out a summons for the minor offense of fishing without a license, dating it for a court appearance at a much later date and time in the summer. I politely advised him, that if he were to purchase a fishing license prior to the assigned court date, I'd gladly withdraw turning the summons in and it would save him the funds he needed to support his family. If he couldn't purchase the required permit prior to the assigned court date, he'd have to make the appearance before the district court judge and face the consequences.

He wisely read between the lines. I was offering him a deal he really couldn't refuse. But after all, if he bought a license as required, he could then fish all he wanted and wouldn't have to pay a fine. In the end, the department would get their money from the license sales and justice would have been well served. I wasn't at all surprised when a few days later he pulled into my dooryard, proudly displaying the required fishing permit as he'd promised to do. He humbly apologized for the embarrassing incident, hoping he hadn't put me in a bad spot.

In the next breath, he asked about the hunting accident from two years earlier, inquiring if we ever found out who the shooter was? I told him we had a prime suspect but that the trail had gone dry as far as having enough evidence to proceed any further.

"I think I might know who the shooter is," he sheepishly stated. In those next few minutes, he provided most of that vital information I'd been seeking in order to bring the investigation to a proper ending. Surprisingly, it didn't involve the prime suspect that for the past two years we investigators had convinced ourselves was the real culprit we were searching for. A good lesson learned, not to prejudge and form an opinion in cases such as this, without the concrete evidence to back up the claim. In this particular incident, after several hours of interviews, private talks, and investigative work, the information kept bringing us back to a home located directly across the highway from where the victim had been shot.

Two days after the first incident, another shooting occurred involving that individual's home. This time a bullet was fired from behind the house, with the projectile entering through the house walls embedding itself into the living room a few feet from a living room chair where moments before the suspect's wife had been seated. The caliber of the bullet removed from the living room wall, appeared to be the same caliber as the firearm used in the incident across the street.

A combination of events coming from this newest investigation, left us highly suspicious of the man of the house possibly being involved in both shooting incidents. He claimed to have been working on both days of these incidents, when in reality he hadn't been. He had lied to us about hunting in the local area on the day of the original shooting, when we could easily prove that he had been in the area with a couple of his buddies. Hoping to get a final resolution to the intense investigation we offered the suspect a lie-detector test, which he agreed to take in order to help prove his defiant innocence. However, on the day of the test, I arrived at his residence, offering to take him to the test area, only to have him backtrack on the offer, claiming he decided he wasn't about to take the test after all. By this time, after constantly being lied to by this individual, we were left with the impression that somehow he was involved in the shooting of the hunter directly across the highway from where he lived, but there was no way of proving it.

The case was placed on the back burner with nowhere else to turn. Now here it was some two years later and I find myself speaking to a young man with very little personal knowledge of the original shooting incident, stating that he thinks he knows who the shooter was. "You don't have to tell me," he stated, "but did your shooter just happen to have been using a .300 Savage rifle, and by any chance did you find an old green hat near the scene?" he calmly inquired.

Needless to say, only myself and two other investigators knew about the caliber rifle and the hat being collected as evidence, so my interest in what he was saying immediately piqued. "What makes you say that?" I calmly inquired, not wanting to confirm or deny his inquiry.

"Well...," he hesitated. "At that time I was working for the railroad. My foreman used to bring his rifle to work with him every day. It was a .300 Savage," he related. "We worked for the railroad replacing tracks and rails along the Belfast/ Moosehead run. Often times we were right out there in prime deer country." he explained. "Our foreman always wore a dirty green hat," he stated. "But the day after that shooting he arrived at work sporting a brand new green hat and no rifle!" he anxiously sputtered. "He told all of us, that from that day on, we no longer were allowed to bring firearms to work! He was really acting quite nervous and very strange. He wouldn't tell us the reasons for the sudden changes," the young man calmly stated. "Ever since that day, I just wondered if perhaps he was somehow involved in that shooting. His actions just seemed like a strange turn of events, and especially to have happened the very next day after that poor guy was shot and left lying there to fend for himself," he said. "All this time I've kind of wondered if perhaps he had something to do with that incident?"

Without a doubt, this newly-acquired information was just the break we needed to solve what, up until then, had been the only unsolved hunting incident remaining in the state. Upon hearing this young man's story, I suddenly realized we'd been pursuing and concentrating on the wrong man. Now by a stroke of sheer luck, it appeared that maybe this case could be resolved after all. Hunter Safety Officer, John Marsh, and I confronted this individual the very next day. Within a matter of minutes

John was given a complete confession. The shooter admitted to panicking and fleeing the scene after firing the shots and hearing the men screaming. For those past two years he claimed he couldn't sleep well, reliving that moment over and over in his mind. In the end, he was quite relieved to have finally owned up and taken responsibility for his mistake. His biggest fear was wondering just when we would be knocking on his door and charging him for his own misgivings. He was truly glad it was finally over! The burden of knowing what he had done was so terribly wrong and keeping it to himself, mentally had taken its toll on the elderly man. Finally having it all out in the open was a tremendous relief. He was willing to take whatever punishment was directed his way. A few weeks later this investigation was satisfactorily closed to all of the parties involved. It would still have been an open case, had it not been for giving a young fisherman a break at a time when he needed it most. But the real purpose of delivering an occasional deer carcass to the needy was not an attempt to simply solicit information, instead it was an honest attempt intended to help those who were in need of a little help, and nothing more.

The importance of developing informants

Many of these local folks apparently had somewhat accepted my presence within their community. I seriously spent a lot of time trying to create a sense of trust and friendship between us, hoping to develop a list of trusted informants. Without the aid of informants, an officer was pretty well out-on-his-own and for all practical purposes he was rather useless. Along with that friendship and trust came a steady flow of information regarding a few of those folks who were committing violations throughout the district. Happily, I was being paid by the public to do my job. Finally some of these people were willing to assist me in those efforts. During the course of 1973, it was frequently reported throughout the community that a few of the so-called "Burnhamites" were illegally killing and selling deer to select customers year-round. In the fall many illegally harvested deer were sold to nonresident hunters coming into the area for the fall hunt. The bigger the buck and the larger the rack of antlers, the more these hunters would pay. Parading their quarry around their home base and relaying a fabricated story regarding the great hunt that bagged the big boy, gave some of them that macho feeling in amongst their long-time buddies who were clueless as to the real story.

I can recall a couple of times when these poachers sold a few of their prized catches to undercover game wardens. Undercover game wardens posing as nonresident hunters. The best story I remember was at a time when two guides from a local sporting camp seized an opportunity to take advantage of my presence during a search for one of their sports – a nonresident hunter who was lost in the big woods where they had placed him earlier that day. This sporting camp was as shady as they come. Many of the guides hired by the owner were verified poachers from the region.

Using information that I secretly had obtained from an insider at the camp was good enough for the department to invest in an undercover sting operation at the hunting lodge, by sending two highly-skilled undercover wardens into the facility, posing as nonresident hunters.

During this particular search for the lost hunter in what was a miserable rainy and cold night, these two intoxicated guides advised me that they were going to head over to another road quite some distance away from where we were searching, to see if possibly their missing client may have taken a series of woods roads and had exited the woods in a different direction than where he was expected to come out. I told them to simply go ahead, mostly just to get them out and away from the area we were searching. It was obvious from their actions, that they didn't want me hanging around there searching for one of their own. But now that they knew exactly where I was at, they seized the opportunity by heading to another section of town, where instead of searching for their missing client, they shot a monster buck spotted with a bright light feeding underneath an apple tree in south Unity.

Sneaking their illegal quarry back to the hunting lodge, they quickly dressed it off, while bragging loudly to those shady clients seated at the lodge's bar, about wisely pulling a fast one on yours truly. The intoxicated bar hoppers all chuckled at their cleverness of seizing a golden opportunity to poach a deer, knowing exactly where the local warden was. One of the undercover wardens hearing their story, wisely suggested, "Hell, maybe you guys should plan on having more lost hunters!" which brought about another loud burst of laughter.

Upon securing the buck on a game poll out in the woods behind the lodge, they offered the hunters staying at the lodge to sell them the critter for a whopping $225. One of the undercover wardens quickly seized upon the opportunity by purchasing the deer for evidence, after dickering the price down to $200. Their proud claim of taking advantage of the game warden who was still searching for one of their own sports, provided this warden with great pleasure and a big smile on my face when several weeks later I was able to officially charge them for two very serious violations. One for selling deer, and the other for possession of a deer killed in the night time. Both violations came with hefty penalties and a little jail time. More importantly, it revoked their guide's licenses forever.

I remember well, the wise smirk on their faces, claiming I'd never convict them of this false information that they figured I was so heavily depending upon. That cocky attitude quickly changed when I smartly stated, "I hate to tell you boys, but that $200 you got for that old buck… Well when you sold it to that nonresident sport seated at your bar… A real wise man, who actually dickered the price you asked down from the $225 to $200! Well boys, that sport was an undercover game warden, who had been living and partying with you people for a few days," I chuckled. "Well the story that he gets to tell an upcoming jury is going to be terrific for a trial, if and when you have one!" I snickered.

Suddenly I saw the color draining out of their faces, when they finally realized that their goose was cooked. Justice did actually work in that particular instance! Thanks to the welcomed information from a well-groomed informant who was willing to assist this warden in shutting this entire operation down, once and for all. Most of these people who eventually became informants, appeared to be genuinely concerned about the illegal activities they were reporting, and more so the detrimental effect it could have on our wildlife resources. However, there were a few of these individuals who willingly were providing information on others, that were simply seeking revenge on someone with whom they had an ax to grind. For them, managing to anonymously get that person into big trouble with the law would more than satisfy their intentions for bringing the information forward.

Amazingly, there even were a few informants who personally got a thrill by pretending to play the role of a cop themselves. They loved reporting illegal activity to an officer and then watching it unfold as the culprits were held accountable for their sins. These individuals were on their own agenda. Quite often they themselves were doing the exact same thing that they were complaining others were doing. It was a territorial turf-struggle of sorts, where some of these folks had staked claim to a territory that they wanted to remain entirely for themselves. Anyone who invaded that particular area was a threat to their own illegal activities.

As a prime example, one day Jack from Troy loudly squawked about Arthur from Thorndike taking far more than his legal limit of smelts from the Bither Brook smelt run. Supposedly, Arthur was filling his containers with the legal two-quart limit of smelts and then stuffing his chest waders full of the small silvery fish afterward. Arthur bragged to his buddies about conveniently walking past "that stupid game warden," with a whole bunch of illegal fish hidden in his waders. Jack felt Arthur was way too brazen about his illegal activities, so he decided to squeal on him. A few nights later with this information in mind, I apprehended Arthur as he once again sauntered past my location with what he claimed to be his legal limit of smelts.

Nonchalantly, I followed him up into the parking lot and away from his buddies, where I asked to check his limit of smelts just as he was about to get into his car. He was extremely calm and cooperative right up until that shocking moment when I asked him to drop his waders. My request for Arthur to drop his waders, was my own version of a smelt-brook strip search. The sweat immediately began running down Arthur's brow as he offered every excuse possible for not wanting to drop his waders. Sure enough, as he slowly lowered the waders, the small silvery fish were clinging from the top of his pants all the way down to his feet, putting him well over the legal limit of smelts that were allowable by law.

"They must've fallen from my net and into my waders, John," he sheepishly stated.

Grinning ever so coyly, I said, "Obviously, they did, Arthur! Obviously, they did!" As I wrote Arthur up for the violation, he said, "John, can I tell you something about Jack from Troy?" he sputtered. "Do you realize he's bragging about taking over his limit of fish out of here almost every night and he tells everybody about it!" he went on. "He stashes hidden containers of smelts well away from the brook, planning to pick them up later on, after he figures everyone has left, including you. Then he returns back to the brook and starts netting them all over again! He is slaughtering the smelt population, John!" Arthur disgustedly sputtered. Listening to Arthur rag on Jack, I just shook my head in total disbelief as I thought, "If you only knew, Arthur, if you only knew that it was Jack who turned you in!"

A few nights later, I located Jack's hidden containers of smelts at the end of the camp road, exactly where Arthur said they'd be. Just as Arthur had promised, Jack arrived during the wee-morning hours to retrieve his cache. I was leaned up against his vehicle waiting for him when he returned with the illegal load. Needless to say, once the legalities were over, both Jack and Arthur continued chumming around together, and I was labeled as the real villain for holding them both accountable for their sins. If they only knew! If they only knew, the real story. That was the way it was with some of these informants.

Obviously, there'd been a little rivalry of sorts between these two men and I apparently became the means of retaliation in settling the score for both of them. In the end, I knew that neither of them could ever be fully trusted, but I also knew that in this instance their information had been good!

In another incident, a young man from Kennebec County purchased an illegally-harvested deer from a local Burnham poacher. He paid for the animal with a personal check, one that lacked the sufficient funds to cover the document. As a means of sending a message that deceitfulness among crooks wouldn't be tolerated, the seller kicked the crap out of the poor guy, sending him to the hospital. Because of his injuries, I was called to investigate the matter and to prosecute the seller. In this case, the victim willingly became my informant, seeking revenge for his injuries against Roger. Roger boasted, "It was worth every gawd-damn penny of the fine I was assessed. No one screws me and gets away with it." Roger showed no remorse for what he'd done. I wondered just what kind of a relationship might exist from there on, between this informant and the man who'd beaten him so severely.

On another case, my informant desperately wanted to end his brother-in-law's illegal business of killing and selling deer. Obviously, there was no family loyalty, or love lost between these two. The informant agreed to introduce an agent of the department posing as a nonresident hunter to his brother-in-law. They quickly secured a large buck for $125. This deer had been shot underneath a light the night before on the outskirts of Unity village. After taking possession of the eight-pointer, we immediately obtained an arrest warrant for Ron rounding him up the next day for the illegal violations. He was charged for illegally selling deer and for killing one after dark. The informant had remained nameless in the request for the warrant. He purposely was protected in the affidavit so as not to reveal his identity for introducing the undercover agent to his brother-in-law.

However, a few nights later and after a few drinks, my informant foolishly bragged about what he'd done. The end result was yet another thumping by the bad guy to the good guy, and another person was sent off to the hospital. So much for family love! I could only imagine what their family reunions must've been like in the months following this melee.

1973 was also the year when that local sporting camp located near my Burnham residence was infiltrated by a couple of undercover wardens posing as nonresident hunters. At my request, they discovered just how illegal this sporting operation was. The illegal deer drives and many other daytime violations, along with the paid night-hunting excursions down the Sebasticook River between Burnham and Clinton via canoe, were just some of the illegal attractions for those staying at the facility. I'd developed a lengthy list of information from an inside informant regarding the illegal activities at this so-called highly respectable public sporting camp. I'd suspected these folks of being rather dishonest long before, but proving it had been futile. In the end, prove it we did, and then some.

The camp was permanently closed and disbanded. Several employees who guided for the owner of the facility were convicted for illegal activities. Justice prevailed, and word rapidly spread throughout the area that the free rein enjoyed by these individuals had finally come to an abrupt ending. Relying upon dependable informants to aid me in my duties of protecting the fish and wildlife resources was priceless but having good informants was yet a necessity if I were to be successful.

Occasionally some violator committed a heinous act that resulted in their best buddies turning them in because they were so offended by the illegal activity. Such was the case in the fall of 1973, when an informant advised me to go out behind his buddy's house in Troy where I'd find an illegally set trap with something in it. The trap itself was legal, the fact that it hadn't been tended to for several weeks was the violation.

A neighbor's dog apparently had been caught in the iron-jawed device where it died of starvation. The total disregard of the trapping laws by Phil, laws that required each trap to be physically tended at least once every 24 hours, was quite obvious. The brutality and cruel death of this gentleman's poor dog was a bit more than what my informant could stand. "That poor creature died a slow and miserable death," he said. "If only Phil had tended his sets like he should have, none of this would've happened."

Phil was ordered into court for the violation. I listened to every excuse in the world why he couldn't check the trap. In this situation, no excuse was acceptable. I still shudder at the thoughts of how that poor dog must've suffered. This was a case of where the informant placed a civil obligation above friendship, and in doing so he may have prevented a similar situation from occurring in the future. Every police officer depends upon a variety of informants during their careers. Without them, the job of a law enforcement officer would be extremely difficult and tedious.

I find myself chuckling today as I look back upon some of the fiascos I found myself involved in, thanks to the support of a community willing to assist me in carrying out those duties. There definitely were some real good informants - those offering up information without a goal or an agenda of their own. They were folks who recognized a responsibility to protect the fish and game resources around them.

Then there were those mediocre informants - those who half-heartedly believed in what they were doing and who did so with a personal agenda in mind. Finally, there were informants who simply ratted out an acquaintance for no good reason other than to seek revenge. It was a guessing game trying to figure out who was whom, and what information was real, or which information might be a little exaggerated. Harvesting and utilizing informants was extremely vital to the profession I'd chosen. Without those informants there wouldn't have been much of a career, and with them, I had more than my fair share of excitement. It was imperative however that an officer provide his informant with full anonymity, never disclosing who they were, even if it meant losing a good case. If the informant wasn't protected to the full extent possible from the officer, word would spread, and the sources of information would quickly disappear. Maintaining the friendship, the trust and a personal bond with an informant was vital to the profession.

Every Town had its Share of Characters

The dictionary describes a *character* as "the pattern of behavior or the personality found within an individual; his or her moral constitution." Without fail, every town in my patrol area had its own share of memorable characters. They were the folks who, for one strange reason or another, managed to stand out above all of the rest. Many of the characters with whom I became well acquainted seemed to exhibit an attitude of total defiance for most of the laws governing our society. One might say they had a blatant disregard of the rules of the game. These characters were totally oblivious to the consequences of their actions, until they found themselves caught red-handed with their paws in the cookie jar. For these folks, a stubborn attitude wasn't simply ignoring the rules, but more so an attitude whereby they simply didn't care if they disobeyed those rules. They'd worry about the consequences later on. And only then, if they happened to get caught for an infraction.

The total defiance of the fish and wildlife laws introduced me to more than one interesting character during my career. But then again, it was these people whom I found myself dealing with most often. For the most part, I found these characters to be highly likable folks. It was just their disregard of society's rules that made them what they were. Grover, a so-called, "Modern day Robin Hood," of the poaching clan, was just one of these characters. But because of his notoriety throughout Central Maine, as a man who had intimidated and struck a sense of real fear into anyone daring to interfere with his errant disregard of the fish and game laws, Grover was by far one of the more memorable characters I'd get to deal with.

Grover didn't live within my district, but he sure as hell knew every inch of it. I reckon there were more people that knew him than there were who knew me. His reputation as a ruthless deer poacher was well known all over Central Maine and beyond. After receiving several warnings from law-abiding folks living within my district and receiving the same advice from several police officers who had dealt with Grover in the past, I was constantly being told not to turn my back on the area's most noted poacher.

Up until then, I had yet to meet the man face to face. It was only a matter of time before I knew we were to confront each other. When it finally happened, I quickly sized him up as being loud and boisterous, but quite amicable to a certain degree. He was somewhat intimidating, mainly because of his large size and his deep, raspy, voice. Grover had a tendency to talk down to those he was speaking to. He did so in a rather authoritative manner and I could sense from our very first gathering, he thoroughly enjoyed being classified as a notorious poacher. He certainly wasn't doing anything to deny or discredit the rumors. Many folks credited Grover with shooting 100 deer or more per year, most of them under the cover of darkness. Just listening to their countless stories made me wonder if the man ever got any sleep.

But then again, my situation wasn't much better, as I tried, night after night, to catch him and others just like him, in the act of committing their dastardly deeds. The truth be known, after my first official meeting with Grover, I personally respected and rather curiously liked the man. We just happened to be on opposite sides of the fence as to interpreting the reasons for the fish and wildlife rules, that's all.

Grover's reputation of using force and intimidation toward anyone who defied his activities was totally unfounded so far as I could tell. But still the rumors prevailed throughout the Central Maine area, even though I never found anyone willing to say that they'd actually been threatened by the man. I wondered if it wasn't his highly-inflated reputation that made most of these folks believe he was capable of doing them harm. Although my buddies in uniform all claimed he bared a lot of watching.

Over a period of time, however, I found the claims about Grover to be quite exaggerated. It was a classic case of whenever he shot one deer underneath a light, by the time the community heard about it, he had shot 15-20. Not to say he didn't illegally kill far more deer than he should have, because there was no denying that fact. Grover was a poacher – no doubt about it! There were far too many rumors concerning Grover's illegal activities for them not to have some merit, rumors which he never tried to rebut.

My own dealings with the old boy over the years substantiated the fact that he enjoyed his night out-on-the-town quite well. The Modern-Day Robin Hood, a title which he thoroughly enjoyed, referred to his philosophy that no meat was ever wasted. According to him, many folks who were up against hard times actually benefited from his illegal activities when he supplied them with a little extra food for the table. During the course of my career, our paths officially crossed several times.

On some of those occasions, the exchanges between us were quite pleasant and humbling, although a bit taunting towards each other in a friendly sort of way. Other times, we experienced a few knock down drag-outs, mostly a war of words, with tempers rising to the point of nearly boiling over, but never once did it reach the level of where we actually became physical with each other. However, there was a time when we beat on each other's equipment, as we held up traffic during a heated verbal tirade between us, right in the middle of the highway. But that was the closest it ever came to going over the edge – although a member of his party ended up getting a trip to jail as an indirect result of that incident.

We seemingly shared a mutual sense of respect for each other. At times our unexpected actions were quite comical to those people in the area who knew the both of us. In Grover's words, "I like you 10 months out of the year. It's that other two months when I'd just as soon not have you anywhere around," he mumbled, referring of course to the busy hunting season. Without fail, once the hunting season was over, I'd see Grover's vehicle pulling into my dooryard. He expected a cup of coffee, where together for hours we'd rag on each other over how the year had gone. He'd cheer and bloat about what he'd gotten by with right underneath my nose– and likewise, I'd make a few points of my own, when during the season I managed to schedule either him or some of his cronies, for a future court hearing or two.

I actually looked forward to that coffee and the casual meeting after the hunting season. Grover was just another example of the many interesting characters I'd get to meet in my profession. But by far, he was one of my most memorable. There were many, many more. Each of them had their own special traits and personalities.

Take Big Jim, from the town of Troy. Now Jim was a highly unusual chap, just because of his size alone. You see, Jim stood 6 feet 2 inches tall and tipped the scales at well over 500 pounds. His unkempt beard and large round face gave him the appearance of being a giant among giants. I knew my chances of ever being in a foot chase with Jim were slim, but my dealing with him were not. I recall joking with him one day about the possibilities of chasing him out through a field some night after he had just blistered a big buck underneath a bright light. "Hell John, I'd have to eat a big box of ex-lax during the day to be fully ready, just in case you decided to chase me at night," he chuckled.

His humorous statement certainly needed no explanation. I really didn't even want to think about it! The chances of Jim ever fleeing on foot were slim at best, no pun intended! I could plan on running across Jim and his cohort, Alan, every fall. Without fail, I'd usually find them in one compromising situation or another. Jim was a character alright. He always seemed to be jovial, slow-moving, highly manipulative and sly as a fox. These are just a few of the words I'd use to describe the giant of a man.

I first met Jim and Alan working in the woods along Unity Plantation. Alan was doing all the hard labor while Jim maneuvered the skidder to and from the yard. Jim had a rather plush job compared to the hard work Alan was tackling. It was a sight to behold, witnessing Jim filling the entire cage of the mechanical monster, which made the machine look like some sort of a Tonka toy. The two of them together made a good pair. They were like two peas in a pod – wherever you found one, you'd find the other. What one couldn't think of, the other one could!

I vividly recall an occasion when I had Jim in court for a series of violations. The judge found him guilty of the charges, assessing a hefty fine. The judge granted Jim a period of time to pay the fines off, along with a stern warning that he would be arrested if he didn't settle his debt with the State of Maine in full within the time frame the judge had allowed.

As usual, Jim neglected to fulfill his obligations to his honor. The judge angrily issued an arrest warrant, demanding that I immediately hunt down and seize possession of the giant, bringing him to the Waldo County Crowbar Hotel. I spent the next few days searching for my buddy. It was quite obvious he knew I was in hot pursuit and what I wanted, as he did whatever he possibly could to avoid the inevitable. Several times I stopped by his residence, knowing full well that more than likely he was sitting inside, but he wouldn't make his presence known. The task turned into a regular cat and mouse game. I was that cat in pursuit of a large mouse that was definitely trying to stay one step away from me.

It was only a matter of time before I'd score a bullseye. Through one of my police sources, I had heard Jim's prized and expensive chain saw had been stolen from the woodlot where he and Alan had been working. More than likely, it was taken by someone Jim owed a little money to and it was now being held as collateral. Especially seeing it wasn't only the courts who never received their owed money. Armed with this little tidbit of information, I devised a hastily put-together plan.

I went to Jim's house to make another nuisance appearance. Like so many times before, his highly-trained wife rather disgustedly claimed he wasn't there, and she didn't know when he'd be back. I knew damn well he probably was perched in the next room smiling like a young virgin exiting a house of ill-repute after having had a rewarding visit.

Upon departing the residence, I beat feet to the Pittsfield Police Department, where Jim's stolen chainsaw report had been taken. I had a plan that just might lure the big boy out of his secure home and into the backseat of my cruiser. At the police department, I removed my own dilapidated chainsaw from the trunk of my cruiser and dragged it into the police station. The patrolman on duty jokingly said, "Are you going to cut the trees down around here, John?"

"Nope, I'm going to execute an arrest warrant. And, hopefully you'll help me do it," I sputtered. I then proceeded to explain my dealings with Big Jim and his little game of playing hide and go seek in order to avoid the warrant. I asked the patrolman to call Jim's house. Obligingly, the young officer made contact at the home where he too was bluntly told by Jim's wife, "He isn't here right now and I don't know when he'll be back. Can I leave a message for him?" she grumbled.

Following the script as planned, the young officer advised her how he'd just recovered a chainsaw from a residence in Pittsfield. "It possibly could be the one Jim reported stolen a while back. Jim needs to come to our station to identify it just as soon as possible, or else we're going to have to return it to the person we seized it from," she was advised.

Her attitude suddenly changed. Anxiously she said, "I know where I can reach him. Just as soon as I do, we'll be right up," she excitedly told the young cop.

"That's great," said the officer. "We need to clear this matter up as soon as possible."

With a big grin on my face, the wait was on. Big Jim had swallowed the bait – hook, line and sinker. Soon he might end up in the tank, and I didn't mean the fish tank! I grabbed the arrest warrant and quickly ducked into a small office, well out of sight, waiting for big Jim to arrive.

Exactly as planned, the old pickup truck, listing heavily to one side from the excessive weight of my hefty friend, came skidding into the parking lot. Big Jim slowly maneuvered himself out of the vehicle with his wife toting along a few feet behind him, just like a puppy following its master. They rapidly shuffled across the parking lot and into the police station. I secretly watched as the young officer greeted them in the lobby. He was holding my old blue chainsaw in his hands.

"That ain't my gawd-damned chain saw," Jim disgustedly grumbled. "Mine is a good one and not a cheap mongrel like that frigging old piece of junk," he sputtered. "Besides, mine is a Husqvarna – and they're all orange, not blue," he continued ranting.

I quickly stepped into the room where they were gathered. With a rather shocked expression on his face, Jim looked my way and smiled, "I think I've been had!" he wisely smirked. With an even bigger grin on my face, I said, "That you have, Jim. That you have!" as I proceeded to advise him he was under arrest and that we were going to take a ride to Belfast together.

It was a struggle placing the 500-plus pound monster into the back seat of my cruiser, but somehow we managed. The car was riding mighty low as we struck out for the long ride to the Waldo County slammer. Along the way we joked about what had transpired and how he kind of suspected there was a trap being set for him, but he didn't dare not check it out, just in case the police had recovered his chain saw.

This wasn't the last time our paths would cross. As a matter of fact, many years later there was an incident where I could write an entire book on the story in itself. A case where I, as the county's elected Sheriff, ended up going to Alaska to extradite Jim back to Maine on one of the more serious charges of his criminal career. That trip alone, was one I called the "trip from hell." If anything could go wrong along the way, it did!

We had to buy Jim two tickets to fit his huge carcass on board the aircraft, and that was after doing a test run on the plane to see if he could fit in the bathroom. If he couldn't we weren't flying! Thank God, at least he made it through that part of the journey. The rest of the trip was a living hell.

Jim was one of those town characters I'd continue running across all through my warden's career and beyond. While he was just a little more distinguished than some, he was still very likable in his own sort of way. I shouldn't admit it, but I surely enjoyed every one of these characters, as one by one they became welcomed additions to the diaries. After all, if it hadn't been for them, I would have been denied what I considered to be job security. One thing about it, my job was quite secure without a doubt!

Big Jim, yet another town character....

Who was the Most Memorable Character?

As I travel around the state promoting my books, speaking about that great career I was able to enjoy, oftentimes I'm asked, "Who was the most memorable character you had to deal with during your employment, John? And what made them so memorable? There were so many of these so-called memorable characters, but without a doubt, I'd list Grover as perhaps being the most challenging and interesting.

Every fall, I planned on butting heads with the old boy, chasing him and the gang from one fiasco to another. Yet we had a strange sort of mutual respect for one another. One where once the dust had settled and the hunting season was over, we could share that cup of coffee and reminisce about that particular fall's ups and downs. Grover would boast about the many things he and the boys got away with, and likewise, I'd remind him of those occasional court appearances where we shared a few memorable moments together in the halls of justice. I never took his activities personally and he was fully aware of it. "I have a job to do Grover, and I fully intend to do it!" I reminded him more than once.

Each little confrontation had different results and quite often a different attitude from Grover and his team, depending upon the circumstances at the time. Grover once stated on the Q-T, "If you catch me fair and square, I'm going to fight you all the way in the courtroom, but I won't resist you in the field!" he sputtered. "But if you railroad me in any way, I'm not saying what will transpire," he quickly warned.

"If you aren't breaking any laws Grover then you have nothing to worry about. It's not our job to railroad anyone!" I rather boldly replied. And so the saga of Grover, the most notorious of the outlaws, and myself as the game protector, began. Out of the many characters I found myself dealing with, he by far was a book in itself. I think it was because of his highly noted reputation alone that I found him to be among the most intriguing and challenging of any of the other characters I met. Read on, as I relate a few of those old memories. The good, the bad, and the sometimes damn right ugly!

That Modern-Day Robin Hood Named Grover

As a new warden traveling throughout my assigned district in 1970, I was desperately attempting to learn the area and its people before the hunting season was to begin. As I traveled around the area, I met several folks who were very receptive to having a new game warden coming into their territory. Almost without fail, many of those in a casual conversation often inquired, "Have you met Grover yet?"

"Who to heck is Grover?" I would curiously ask. They quickly explained that Grover was an alleged and notorious poacher who roamed freely throughout the area. His reputation was that of being a bad character. One that should require using extreme caution upon approach. Although these comments were strictly rumors with nothing factually backing them up, it seemed to be a topic of conversation that came up with just about everybody I met. They labeled Grover as an intimidating and ruthless poacher, operating with an attitude of total defiance to society's laws. Especially those regarding the fish and wildlife rules.

Grover's loud and boisterous voice obviously had instilled a real sense of fear into many of these law-abiding folks – people who supposedly at one time or another had personally run across the man. I was strongly warned, "If you attempt to stop Grover, or any of his ruthless gang, don't turn your back on them John! They'd just as soon shoot you as not!" they advised.

I had to admit, these well-meaning words of caution from so many folks that I didn't really know, created a personal concern in my mind. Especially considering the fact I was just beginning my professional career in an area already noted for its violence against the local warden, after some local thugs shot the windows out of the warden's camp where my predecessor lived with his wife and young daughter. Those ruthless thugs committed the dastardly act, while the young warden's wife and infant daughter lay huddled together on the floor of the small state-owned camp, fearing for their lives.

With this new information on my mind, I made a few inquiries from the police agencies around the area, asking if any of them were aware of this character named Grover. Not surprising, all of them were well aware. They too issued the same warnings and cautions that I was getting from the public, "You really want to be on guard and watch your back John if you run across any of them!" they boldly advised this rookie warden.

Most of Grover's associates also had highly questionable reputations of their own. The entire gang was well known throughout the Central Maine area for their rampant crime sprees and other occasional illegal activities. The main culprits seemed to hail from the Vassalboro, Waterville and Winslow areas of Central Maine. They all had, at one time or another, experienced more than their fair share of run-ins with the local law enforcement agencies, whether it was the local police, the game wardens, sheriff's deputies or the state police. Every department seemed to know them. And they seemed to know them well!

Whenever a major crime occurred locally, their names always seemed to rise to the top of the list as prime suspects. More often than not they were somehow involved, but usually smart enough to avoid any serious repercussions. This supposed gang of outlaws consisted of Grover, Dickey, Bobby, Moe, Mavel and a few others who all chummed around together. The hunting season was the most popular time of the year for the gang to congregate as a team. During this time, Grover's tribe was enhanced by a group of out-of-state associates who themselves were not regarded as being the most law abiding of citizens. According to the rumor mill, Grover was the leader of an alleged poaching ring that supposedly killed more than 100 deer a year. These illegally killed deer were reportedly sold, bartered, or given away to friends or other associates. Without

A collection of some of Grover's gang. What a tribe they were!

fail during my travels, more than one humble citizen told about not daring to report the illegal activities involving any of them that was occurring in their neighborhoods. There was a genuine fear of retaliation by the gang if they were to do so. Many people stated, to be labeled a snitch by Grover and the gang, instilled enough intimidation and fear in the neighborhood, causing most people to look the other way.

After hearing all of these comments it was obvious folks felt as if Grover and his gang were untouchable by law enforcement. Especially in preventing or slowing down their illegal hunting practices. More than once I was told, "The word around here is that you fellows are afraid of them yourselves!" I was advised. I desperately tried to assure them all that I'd taken an oath to uphold and enforce the laws of our state. I wouldn't differentiate between Grover or any other citizen who violated those rules.

"He may have a bad reputation and he may have instilled a real sense of fear for many of you folks, but I assure you, I will deal with those situations when they arise," I enthusiastically explained.

In my mind I was hoping that when and if the time came, that it would turn out for the best. I actually found myself somewhat dreading that time when I actually might meet up with this group, especially out on some back road in the middle of the night, realizing just how much they despised the duties I was legally required to perform. I also knew that if I were to show even the slightest signs of fear or intimidation, it would be the worst thing I possibly could do. I'd resolved myself into dealing upfront with the matter whenever, and if, it happened. After all, if I got pounded, there were 119 and more of us statewide who would come to the aid. I decided I would treat them the same way I'd treat anyone else under the same circumstances. The final results and the manner of treatment they'd receive in return, would be entirely up to them.

Some folks actually viewed Grover as a modern-day Robin Hood of sorts, "Stealing from the state and giving to the poor!" There was no doubt in my mind that Grover and his crew had created a definite sense of fear and intimidation upon a wary public. One that spread throughout my district and beyond. Grover's occupations and interests varied. Besides hunting and fishing, he was quite active in other duties and enjoyment.

During the off-season from hunting, if he ever acknowledged there was such a time, he served as a bouncer at a couple of bars located in the Waterville-Winslow area. During the day, when he wasn't off hunting, he worked by himself as a wood cutter, utilizing a team of work horses to do the heavy workload. Grover relied upon his team of horses to harvest wood the old-fashioned way, disregarding the modern technology of utilizing a skidder to do the heavier work. The manual labor of working in the woods by hand, day after day, added sheer muscle and agility to his already large 6-foot-plus frame. That extremely deep and intimidating voice was all by itself an attention getter!

I knew it was only a matter of time before our paths would cross, either professionally or during a general conversation somewhere. On one hand, I rather anxiously anticipated meeting this modern-day Robin Hood of the Poaching Community, although I was wondering just how that meeting would go! I hoped we might establish a form of mutual respect and rapport between us. One that would set the ground rules for the many years to come.

It wasn't long before we had a chance to observe one another from a short distance away, while I was out on patrol. We occasionally passed each other sailing along the highways, as we were heading in opposite directions. I'd been on special alert, watching out for that robin's egg blue GMC truck Grover supposedly was driving. The old battered truck had many wounds from one end to the other, the results of the rough journey it had been exposed to over a period of time. Whenever we met, we kind of gave each other the evil-eye as we passed along the highway. I'd signal to Grover a friendly wave of the hand as a sign of friendship, yet letting him know I was quite aware of just who he was. Grover often returned the salute, although I couldn't quite tell if he was using all five of his large fingers.

Nonetheless, as of yet, we hadn't experienced that face-to-face confrontation that I knew was only a matter of time before happening. It was inevitable. From what I was hearing, Grover's attitude toward killing deer was quite simple. He felt by taking a few now and then and giving them to the poor, was nothing more than robbing from the state to assist those who needed a little help fending for themselves and their families. This theory may have sounded good in principle, but for the most part, the facts didn't seem to back up the real philosophy of his activities! Rumor had it, one of Grover's favorite sayings whenever he flashed a blinding light out into a dark field in the middle of the night was, "If it's brown – it's down!" Meaning if the wild critter spotted underneath the bright light was brown, the loud crack of a rifle shot would more than likely reduce it to his possession.

In the early fall of 1970, I finally had that first encounter with the old boy. It happened strictly by chance during a stop I'd made at a local garage in Unity. I was in the process of making yet another one of my many emergency runs to the local garage after poking a large hole in the muffler of my cruiser, seriously damaging the oil plug. Quite often I found myself cruising down some old back road that I didn't belong on, as I was attempting to learn the large area comprising my new patrol. I often found myself cruising off onto a back road that even a skidder would have hesitated to travel over. John Hubbard, the owner of the little garage who bailed me out of so many mechanical catastrophes, looked forward to my many unscheduled visits. In a sense, my visits were a welcomed sign of job security for his little establishment. He knew that my travels out into the back country were primed for keeping his business afloat. John was quite adamant that whenever I needed his services, to simply pull into the station. No appointment was ever needed! I was always given a top priority preference.

John and his wife Thelma operated the small business as a team. These great folks had kind of taken me under their wings like a little duckling from the very first day I arrived in town. They both appeared to enjoy having me hanging around. But then again, why wouldn't they? I definitely was a real asset to their business. Almost daily I had to have some slight overhaul done on my cruiser. The results of trying to reach out into places where even God hadn't traveled for quite some time. I hate to admit it, but I kind of operated under the warped philosophy of nickel and diming my state-issued cruiser to death. Occasionally, just for good measure, I'd throw in a quarter or fifty-cent piece, while trying to access one of those remote areas I was too damned lazy to walk over.

On this particular day, as I entered the garage I noticed a large-framed man loudly doing all the talking with John and Thelma standing there, doing all the listening. The conversation consisted of the normal chit-chat, while John busily completed some repair work on the old blue GMC pickup truck that I immediately recognized as Grover's. Grover's truck was in the same dented and banged up condition as my cruiser had been experiencing. Both vehicles had dead grass and brush hanging from the undercarriage and both of them were completely covered in dried mud. They were scratched from one end to the other. It was difficult to say whose wagon was torn up the most, but in reality Grover's looked a little rougher than mine. It was obvious however, that we both had been traveling into similar territories.

As I entered the garage, Grover intensely stared in my direction, immediately ending his conversation. There was no sign of a smile on his face, but instead, a sort of irritated look of sheer intimidation and defiance cast my way. Sporting a big grin on his face, John, the owner of the little garage said, "Grover, this is John Ford our new game warden. Have you had a chance to meet him yet?" he chuckled. It was obvious from that devious smirk on John's face, that he was thoroughly enjoying this moment in time. John liked watching someone squirm in a time of stress or just before a little confrontation of sorts.

Now standing before him, was the area's most talked about bad guy and the lawman who one day could be confronting him. The introduction was a bit awkward for both of us, as I slowly walked over to Grover, offering to shake his hand. With a forced grin of my own, I bravely said, "I certainly have heard a lot about you Grover! I'm sure some damn glad to finally be meeting you."

"I'll bet you've heard a lot!" Grover said with a loud laugh, "You don't want to believe everything you hear, you know," he shouted.

"I don't," I sputtered. "Only time will reveal the truth from all the rumors," I rather nervously smirked. Grover had a fairly deep voice and a distinct chuckle that could be heard for miles around. Especially whenever he made a comment that to him was an important statement, followed by a wise crack at the end. He'd chuckle loudly, proud of himself for having made his point while making sure that those around him heard it.

With the ice finally broken, we began talking about the many deer showing up in the area. It wasn't too long before he voiced his total disgust with the management practices and the fish and game department as a whole. Grover appeared to be quite knowledgeable regarding the habits and condition of the deer and moose within our area. But then again, from what I was hearing, he should have been.

"People tell me, that in order to be a good game warden, you had to have been a poacher yourself! That's what they tell me!" he sputtered. "You had to be a poacher yourself in order to know the trades of the business!" he loudly snickered, followed by that little chuckle obviously seeking approval from John and Thelma who were thoroughly enjoying every moment of the conversation they were witnessing.

"Oh, I don't know about that, Grover! I suppose it wouldn't hurt to have had a little inside track and experience, but it wasn't a prerequisite for the job by any means," I laughed. "Perhaps someday, Grover, we can both sit down over a cup of coffee and share our views. I'd be quite interested in hearing yours," I said.

"Sounds good to me," Grover responded. The tension by now was gone, much to the disgruntlement of John, who wanted to continue stirring the pot in the worst way.

Our first meeting had been far more cordial and reasonable than I'd been expecting. Truthfully speaking, I actually kind of enjoyed it. I left the garage that day feeling that perhaps Grover might not be the most honest of individuals around, but certainly I had formed an opinion that he was not the type of dangerous individual that he had been portrayed as. I certainly didn't get the impression that he'd put a bullet in the back of my head if I was to turn my back on him. I honestly thought his reputation had been highly exaggerated and that realistically, he was nowhere near as evil as I'd been warned. I actually found myself liking the man, even though it was quite evident that we both shared different philosophies regarding the fish and wildlife rules.

I really did hope, that one day we could actually sit down for a little one-on-one conversation – a time to share our thoughts and to become a little better acquainted with one another. Grover's knowledge of the out-of-doors was quite intriguing to say the least. At least for now, I could honestly say to those folks who asked: "Have you met Grover yet?"

"Yup, I have! I've met Grover! And I'm sure from what I've seen and heard, we will be meeting again!" I sputtered. And we did! With our initial meeting finally behind us, the next time I happened to meet Grover on the road, his wave seemed to be a little more enthusiastic and genuine. I actually think it included all five of his fingers and he even expressed a slight hint of a smile.

There would be many stories over the years involving Grover and his cohorts. Some were good – and some were bad! But none of them proved to be anywhere as threatening and dangerous as I'd been warned by the public. At least from what I had observed thus far, this dangerous reputation he'd been given just wasn't so!

Capturing Robin Hood and his Merry Men!

On October 29, 1970, Norman Gilbert and I were working in Unity hoping to capture some of those dastardly night hunters who had been frequently hunting the area for the past few nights. At 1:30 in the morning, a pickup truck cruised past the area, flashing a bright beam of light into the fields, obviously searching for a deer. After a brief chase we got the vehicle stopped, the light had been thrown out the window during the chase, but was recovered a short time later. I quickly recognized the robin's egg blue GMC as Grover and his cronies. There was a chance that a firearm may have been thrown out too, but if there was, it was never found. The three men were cited to court for illuminating wild game.

As I wrote up the summonses, I obtained the proper identification from Grover and his pal Bobby, but the third gentleman claimed he didn't have any identification on him. Trusting his honesty, I asked him his name and address and any other information needed for the court summons. Defiantly he stated his name was Lenny Sharpe and that he was from Braintree, Massachusetts.

By then we were all engaged in a rather heated discussion as to why they'd been stopped and were being charged for a violation when they didn't have a light. As professionally as I could, I barked, "Look, I'm not treating you with any disrespect and likewise I don't appreciate your arrogance now. If you think you aren't guilty, show up in court and present your case!" I disgustedly stated as I passed out the three summonses.

Grover grabbed his and in that intimidating voice of his he yelled, "You're *@*- damned right we'll have a trial. This is nothing more than harassment and you know it!!" he yelled, as he shoved the truck into gear and screeched away from the area.

The first official action with Central Maine's notorious poacher gang was in the books, it was time to await that day of reckoning before the magistrate.

A few weeks later, we arrived at the courthouse ready to do battle. Grover and Bobby stood in the hallway as I walked by them, staring at me with an intimidating look of disgust. Lenny was nowhere to be seen. After the brief court trial, Grover and Bob were found guilty of their sins and assessed a small fine. Lenny failed to appear for the trial.

The judge immediately issued a warrant for Lenny's arrest. That is, if anyone knew who he was, or where he might be? For the first time since that early morning encounter, I realized that just maybe old Lenny wasn't who he claimed to be. And how could I prove it now, seeing that I'd taken him for his word that he was who he said he was. Once again, a good lesson learned – never trust the words of someone who you catch in a compromising position when they tell you something without the proof to back it up. Just like I did with old Jimbo on the early trapping case a few weeks before, I trusted Lenny to be telling the truth!

After the trial, Grover looked at me in the hallway, smiling ever so coyly, he winked. "Well you won that one," he chuckled. The defiance he displayed during the initial stop no longer seemed evident, it was almost like he had put on a show for his buddies, but we had established that small sense of mutual respect between us.

However, Grover was quite amused by Lenny Sharpe's failure to appear. "That old Lenny was some gawd-damned sharp wasn't he, John?" Grover smirked. Grover and Bob both knew damned well that Lenny had provided me with a fictitious name - and they loved it. They made that fact quite obvious as they both loudly hee-hawed all the way to Grover's truck when they left the courthouse. I had to laugh right along with them, because truthfully speaking, Lenny had indeed been some damned sharp. But on the other hand, I'd been pretty damned dumb.

I left the courthouse that day, rather cautiously still liking the county's most notorious poacher. Why? I don't know. I didn't take the issue personally, reminding me of that advice I had been given by Verne, so many weeks before. "Don't take the job personally, John, or it will eat you up!"

For now, we seemed to have established a mutual understanding between us. Grover knew I had a job to do, and that I intended to do it. Although our philosophies differed widely, I didn't find Grover nearly as threatening as I'd been warned. "You catch me doing wrong, John, and I'll fight you every inch of the way. But I'll do it in the courts and not give you a hard time out in the field," he had stated. "Just make sure you've got the goods on me, and that you can prove it," Grover boisterously chuckled.

I took him for his word and for the most part, he honored his pledge. In the days following the trial we occasionally met traveling along the highway. I couldn't help but notice that Grover was flipping me the full five-fingered salutation, rather than that one-fingered salute I thought I was receiving before. By golly, I think we actually had a sense of respect for each other.

Call to the Commissioner

During the busy 1971 deer hunting season, I was working with Warden Langdon Chandler. We were patrolling in my district, seeking out violators and answering complaints. I'd received numerous complaints about Grover and a crew of nonresident hunters supposedly gang-hunting in the Jackson/Dixmont area.

Gang-hunting is one of the toughest cases of any to prove in a court of law. There were way too many elements of the crime to properly prove such a case. However, on this day several people were bitterly complaining about this large group of hunters that Grover supposedly was bringing into their neighborhood.

"Sometimes there are 15 or 20 in the group," these folks griped. Of more concern, was the many deer being carted out of the area – deer that supposedly were to be sold? The chances of catching the crew in the act of committing a crime was remote at best. But we decided that perhaps maintaining a constant presence within the area, might deter them from their illegal activities. The chore of locating the gang then became a cat-and-mouse game of sorts. If nothing else, it appeared that at least the local residents were extremely pleased to have us maintaining a presence in their neighborhoods.

Grover always took great pains to hide their vehicles whenever they were hunting in a certain location. They communicated to each other via handheld walkie-talkies,

206

warning one another about anyone in a law enforcement capacity traveling into the area. At the same time they were constantly monitoring the police scanners, trying to determine exactly where we wardens were.

This modern-day Robin Hood and his merry men had certainly gone hi-tech. The entire operation was a well-planned procedure, for sure. Eventually we found Grover's truck hidden in the brush off of a remote back road in Jackson. The gang obviously was somewhere nearby. Scanning the landscape, I spotted a lone hunter standing a short distance away. He was rather intently staring off into the tree line and a small clearing directly in front of him. Close by stood another hunter. He too, seemingly was concentrating on the same area. They both appeared to be waiting for someone coming through the woods.

Chandler headed for one of the men to check licenses and I went for the other. This hunter never heard a thing as I slowly approached him. "Hi there," I said. "I'm the local game warden. Do you have your hunting license right with you?" I inquired. Obviously startled by my presence, his hands shook like a dog passing razor blades as he quickly reached around for his wallet. I recognized him as one of the nonresident hunters who the day before had been traveling with Grover.

"Are you out here by yourself?" I calmly inquired.

"Kind-of," he nervously stated, as he handed his license over for my inspection.

"What do you mean, "kind of?" I quizzed him.

"Well, I've got some friends down there in the woods, I don't know all of their names, but we're kind of hunting together," he nervously sputtered.

"You're not driving deer are you?" I sarcastically inquired.

"Ahhh, oh no, sir! No sir! I believe that's illegal," he sheepishly replied. He obviously was quite uncomfortable with my standing alongside him, as he cautiously responded to my questions.

"Sir, can I tell you something?" he suddenly stuttered. "I'm a federal law officer in Massachusetts, and I really don't want any trouble with you folks up here," he nervously stated.

Rather bluntly, I said, "You gotta be kidding me? For an officer of the law, you sure as hell have picked a damned good crew to be hanging out with," I disgustedly sputtered.

"Look, I know this Grover fella apparently has a bad reputation with you folks, and I know you guys are watching him closely," he stated. "I can't afford to get mixed up in any illegal shenanigans with any of them," he shamefully stuttered.

"Well, I'm not saying there's anything illegal going on here my friend, but I certainly have my suspicions that there very well could be," I informed him. "I plan on hanging around here for a spell. It's my job, and certainly you as an officer of the law know how that works?" I calmly stated.

"That's good enough for me," he groaned, as he quickly unloaded his firearm and headed back to his secluded vehicle. "You won't see me around again!" he stated as he quickly headed for his vehicle parked nearby. The hunter who Warden Chandler was confronting also decided that he too had experienced quite enough for the day, as he joined his buddy back at the car.

We both chuckled a few minutes later when we heard a couple of shots coming from down in the woods. These shots came right from the area of woods where we suspected Grover and the remainder of his crew might have been driving deer. Within minutes, an eight-point buck bounded across the field right where, moments before, the federal agent and his buddy had been perched. I said to Chandler, "Yes-siree, we've just saved that deer from a definite demise!"

I suppose that our actions could've been viewed as being just a little bit on the hunter harassment side. Today as I think about it, I think maybe they were! But this type of enforcement was needed in a case such as this!

Soon Grover and his gang emerged from the woods, quite astonished to find Chandler and I standing where their buddies had been posted earlier. We immediately exchanged a few words. It wasn't a friendly conversation by any means! Grover, in that deep and intimidating voice of his, yelled and screamed about being harassed by the gawd-damned game and fish department! He always referred to the department as, "game and fish," instead of "fish and game."

Grover made it quite clear that he planned to file a formal complaint with the Fish and Game Commissioner, George Bucknam, come Monday morning. He stressed the fact that he was real good friends with the Commissioner and that they had a very stable and close relationship. He loudly grumbled for the benefit of his rowdy buddies, "Heads are definitely going to roll from this *^# - damned *#*!** harassment, bull*#*!" he yelled. "Nothing but gawd damned harassment!" he kept yelling.

Calmly I said, "I'm only trying to do my job, Grover. I wouldn't want to see you getting into any trouble you know." Whatever friendship I figured we'd established prior to that day, appeared to have taken a sudden turn for the worse. I expected, from this point on, that I might be getting that one-fingered salute from the old boy once again.

Holding true to his word, Grover did contact the main office demanding a personal meeting with Commissioner Bucknam. The Commissioner graciously listened to his complaints and concerns. Shortly afterward, I received a direct call from the commissioner, requesting an explanation of my actions and the sequence of events as they'd occurred. "You're doing just right, John! The only thing I ask is that you cover your butt and just be sure you're treating him fairly," George apologetically advised. "He's a little put-out at you right now, but I'm sure he'll get over it," George chuckled. In a subtle kind of way, George said, "I honestly think he really kind of likes and respects you. Probably the man would've made a damn good game warden, had he only been on the other side of the fence," George chuckled.

Sadly, there was some truth to George's statement. Grover certainly was well versed in the many tricks of the trade, and without a doubt he would've made a good warden. Amazingly during the busy hunting season, Grover was out and about as much as I was. I'd often meet him during the day, when I'd pass his severely-dented pickup truck. And then occasionally, we'd meet during the late hours of the night, leaving me to wonder where he'd been, and more so, what he'd been doing? At least I was getting paid for my time and he wasn't. Although, if he sold as many deer as folks claimed he was, without a doubt he was making a hell of a lot more money than me.

After this latest flareup I wondered how things might transpire between the two of us from that point on. I thought about whether I should reconsider those old warnings, perhaps exercising a little more caution if we were to have another confrontation of any sorts. But I really didn't think it was necessary. I also knew Grover was highly upset at many of the game wardens from around the area. So I guess, I wasn't alone! There were some of the wardens that he didn't hesitate voicing his total disgust for. I wasn't exactly sure just where I stood on that list, but I doubted I was exempt!

Time would tell. Surely there'd be many more dealings with the man known as the state's most notorious poacher. I'd have to wait and see how he reacted when the next time arrived, as I knew it would! I knew damn well, he hadn't mended his ways. I reckon it was just my inability to have been in the right place at the right time during that season. But I knew there'd be future encounters waiting by the wayside, when once again we would butt heads.

Tomato Soup, Crackers, and a Visit from the Scout

It was during the 1971 hunting season, November 19th to be exact, when I heard the clanging and banging of a pickup truck pulling into the dooryard of the state-owned warden's camp. I'd made a quick stop at home, seeking a little nourishment, prior to heading out for another long night of hoping to apprehend a night hunter or two.

Much to my surprise, I saw Grover coming up to the door, sporting a big grin on his face. I couldn't help but wonder why I had the honor of having the area's most notorious poacher coming to my doorstep.

"Am I in time for supper?" Grover inquired in that loud, husky, and rather intimidating voice of his.

"You are if you like canned tomato soup and crackers," I laughed. "A poor bachelor like me, doesn't like to cook too much you know. So I make the best out of whatever I can – straight from a can," I laughed. "Canned tomato soup is my favorite during the hunting season. It's easy to prepare and quick to consume," I chuckled. "Did you know you can serve it with crushed crackers while mixing it with water? Or you can prepare it cooked in milk and served with a couple of slices of heavily buttered bread," I snickered. "Occasionally I don't bother mixing it with anything, I simply open the can and devour it," I chuckled.

"You know, it would taste a hell of a lot better if you had a nice slab of fresh deer meat to go along with it," Grover teasingly responded.

"You don't have any to spare, do you?" I sarcastically snickered.

"If I did, you sure as hell would be the last person I'd give it to," he laughed. "I just thought I'd stop by to shoot the breeze with you and to give you a little something. He smiled as he passed over an 8x10 glossy picture of himself kneeling in front of the beat-up pickup truck, holding up a huge buck that he supposedly had bagged earlier.

"If I didn't know better, I'd say it was the same buck I saw running up across the clearing a few days before, when Warden Chandler and I broke up one of your suspected deer drives," I snickered.

"You're guess might be closer than you think," he chuckled.

"What time of the day, or should I say night, did you bag this beauty Grover?" I smiled.

"John, you seriously don't think I'd take it illegally?" he chuckled in that loud boisterous voice that by now had become his trademark. Somehow, I felt this visit was a little bit more than being neighborly, but I certainly wasn't about to accuse him of anything without the facts to prove it. Maybe, just maybe, he was being overly friendly, but I seriously doubted it! I'm sure there was a motive for his being there, other than to leave me wondering where this buck in the photo had come from, and how legal it had been in the taking?

We chatted for a few more minutes about the current hunting season and his recent meeting with the Commissioner. "Did you know that I filed a formal complaint against you with the game and fish department for harassment?" he sputtered.

"I did hear that Grover. I respect that it's your right. Like I told you before, I won't treat you any differently than anyone else, but I have a job to do and I intend to do it," I stated. "Now honestly speaking Grover, certainly you must know with your reputation that you deserve a little more attention than most folks, don't you?" I kind of snickered back.

"Just rumors John, just rumors! Don't believe everything you hear," he chuckled. "I just thought I'd stop by to say hello and see how you're doing. I wanted to be neighborly and hope there are no hard feelings. Not that I've really missed you a hell of a lot," Grover winked, as we slowly walked back outside towards his truck.

By now it was totally dark. I was concerned that any poor deer standing out in an open field after Grover left my house would be fair game for him to take, but what else could I do? There were only so many places I could be at once. The next evening, November 20th, instead of returning home at supper time, I decided to work the late hunters in the south Unity area. I still had it in the back of my mind that maybe the little visit from Grover the previous night might have been a check just to see if in fact I went home for supper.

On this night, I was watching a series of apple trees in an area heavily frequented by deer. I was comfortably perched alone in my cruiser, when I noticed the headlights of a vehicle slowly coming my way. Suddenly a beam of light began sweeping the apple trees all around me, searching for those yellow eyes of a deer feeding upon the fallen apples. My heart started racing, anticipating what the next few minutes might bring. There were no deer in the orchard, as the vehicle slowly passed by my hidden cruiser.

Quickly, I pulled in behind the pickup truck, using their headlights to guide me, as the truck continued along down the narrow country road. Once I was directly behind the vehicle, I initiated the headlights, siren, and the emergency lights, signaling for the driver to stop. As my lights illuminated the pickup truck, I immediately recognized the beat-up old blue pickup truck in front of me as being the one parked in my door yard the night before.

It was Grover's. What were the chances? I could tell it was him behind the wheel, with a friend alongside of him who was as big as, if not bigger, than Grover himself. They both appeared to be heavily engaged in some type of frantic activity inside the vehicle, as they rapidly sped away in an obvious attempt to put a little distance between us.

Suddenly the truck skidded to the side of the road, coming to an abrupt stop. I nearly slammed into it, as I bolted from the cruiser on a dead run, heading for yet another rendezvous with Grover and his gang. Luck was definitely on my side this night. As I approached the two men, Grover's buddy, Tommy, was holding a rifle between his legs, while he repeatedly slammed his arms against the door in an attempt to exit the vehicle.

In his haste to escape from the vehicle, he struck the door lock with his elbow, locking himself inside. Grover, on the other hand, was desperately trying to grab the two rifle shells that were rolling back and forth on the floorboards by his feet. If he could somehow discard those shells, he knew I'd have no case to prove the night hunting offense without ammo.

In his haste, he had accidentally dropped the shells before he could toss them out the window. As I yanked the door of the truck open, I saw Grover still reaching for the shells that were rolling around by his feet. Grover sheepishly looked at me and commented, "Looks like you got yourself a big catch tonight, John!"

Quickly, I placed them both under arrest, "I guess you know what the routine is from here Grover?" I excitedly said. Grover humbly handed over the two shells from the floorboard, as Tommy passed over the rifle. They both were rather sheepishly chuckling and still somewhat griping between themselves as to how unlucky they'd been. Their plan of escape had called for Grover to pitch the live rounds of ammo out the window, discarding any evidence he might have. Tommy, on the other hand, was supposed to jump from the vehicle and run into the woods with the rifle, hopefully preventing me from proving a night hunting charge.

It just goes to show that even the most elaborate of plans sometimes doesn't work. For these boys, this truly was their unlucky night. Fortunately, neither of them gave me a hard time. To the contrary, they both were extremely cordial, especially considering the situation they suddenly found themselves in. "I thought for sure you'd be home eating your tomato soup and crackers," Grover sheepishly smirked.

"Not tonight, Grover! Not tonight!" I replied. "You weren't by chance out here trying to get me a slab of fresh deer meat to go with my soup and crackers, were you?" I couldn't resist joking.

Grover just grinned! "The game and fish department will be some proud of you tonight, John boy!" he sputtered. "You got the big fish tonight!" he chuckled. "But I look at it this way, it's a lot better you than someone else," he deviously snickered. I didn't really know whether to take his comments as a compliment or not, so I just grinned. It was quite obvious, the previous night's visit from Grover was nothing more than a scouting mission. It had been a visit to see if I routinely was at home for supper. There was no doubt about it, the old boy was clever in his mode of operation – this case was no exception.

But on this particular night, luck happened to be on my side in more ways than one! I can't explain it, but somehow I thoroughly enjoyed those occasional dealings with Grover. I treated him with the respect he deserved and, likewise, I seemingly got some of that same respect back. There was no need of damning Grover for constantly breaking the law. He knew exactly what he was doing and he knew the risks involved. After all, if it wasn't for a few folks like him, I wouldn't have had a job.

And once again, this friendly little rivalry between Robin Hood and Little John would continue. As a side note, later after the season had passed, and during Grover's annual after-the-season coffee chats, he was quick to let me know that his trip to jail with Tommy was not in vain.

"What do you mean by that Grover," I inquired.

"Once we made bail, I went to a friend's house in Belfast, where I borrowed one of his rifles," he chuckled. "Tommy and I got two big ones on the way home from jail!" he snickered and belly laughed, wanting me to know the trip hadn't been for naught! Whether they really did or not, I guess I'd never know for sure. But if I had to guess, I'd say the odds were in his favor! It wouldn't be the last time our paths would cross and the saga would continue.

Foot-Jack-Uh!

One of the highlights of my career was persistently pursuing those folks who knowingly committed the most serious of the fish and game violations, that of the almighty night hunter. The penalties for this crime in the 1970s were a mere $200 and the possibility of losing one's hunting privileges for a year. It was a penalty far more lenient than the $1,000 minimum fine, the forfeiture of firearms and any equipment used in the crime, along with a mandatory jail sentence and the automatic revocation of hunting privileges that comes with a conviction today.

But even in those earlier times, $200 was a significant amount of money for most families. For me, the idea of working night after night hoping to capture night hunters was the most exciting part of my job. I thrived on constantly anticipating the unknown and experiencing the excitement of the chase that was a part of the game. And a game it was!

Folks engaging in night hunting knew exactly what they were doing. They obviously were trying to outwit their local warden, and we wardens were trying to be smart enough to rope them in. For the most part, the advantage was entirely theirs.

By far the cagiest of all the night hunters to apprehend, were those who walked into a back field, or an orchard, or some other remote spot near their homes, with a hand-held light and a rifle, carefully and very methodically stalking a white tail out in the open. These "foot-jack-uhs" as I called them, usually dressed warm for the occasion. They were extremely familiar with the countryside they hunted, unlike those lazy nincompoops who chose to hunt from a warm vehicle with a plug-in spotlight, flashing one field after another, hoping to catch a big buck grazing in the black of night.

Instead, the foot-jack-uhs were serious in their efforts, knowing their chances of getting caught were slim at best. If the truth was known, probably most of the so-called heater-hunters were afraid of the dark in the first place. Perhaps they had valid reasons to be a leery of the dark. I recall a few times when I was a little skeptical of it myself. Thus far in my young career, I had yet to capture a "foot-jack-uh."

The closest I'd come was chasing after a night hunter who fled on foot from a remote field in Burnham. As I barreled down across the field, running as fast as my fat little legs would carry me, I found myself rapidly gaining upon my man. It was one of those nights when it was darker than the inside of a rubber boot and another one of those times when I'd failed to grab my flashlight in my haste to get going.

The next thing I knew, I went sailing head-first into the puckerbrush as my legs snagged onto a barbed wire fence located along the wood line. Needless to say, my escapee knew the area far better than I. The last I heard of him, the brush was breaking and crashing far ahead of me as he scurried off into the dark of night and I lay stunned in the muck along the edge of the old grown-up field.

My partner, Norman, was on his way to assist but the effort was useless. Oh well, it was just another one of those cases where sometimes you win a few and sometimes you lose a few. That night, I ended up being on the losing end.

November 12, 1973, however, was a different story. It was a real dark and frosty night as I parked on an old tote road adjacent to the Hemlock Hill Road in Unity. Nearby was a green field that looked rather enticing for someone who was searching for a big buck feeding under the cover of darkness. I'd just poured myself a hot cup of coffee and was settled inside the comfort of my cruiser, watching, waiting, and listening, wondering if this was a good spot, or whether perhaps I should be somewhere else.

Suddenly, I saw a quick burst of light sweeping the field near where I had parked. At first, I thought I might have been seeing things, as my eyes often played tricks on me in the black of night. I quickly turned off the radio and rolled down the window, in hopes of discovering if someone else was lurking nearby. Soon afterward, the beam of light again flashed the nearby field, only this time it appeared to be getting much closer.

My heart started racing, as I anticipated what kind of a mess I'd soon be in. I knew there'd be one, there always was, and it looked like I might be chasing after yet another foot-jack-uh. I slowly exited the cruiser, making sure I had my flashlight gripped tightly in my hand.

The wait was on, as I scanned the darkness hoping to see signs of movement while listening for the rustle of approaching footsteps. I could hear the quiet shuffling of feet slowly heading my way through the darkness. They'd walk for just a short distance and then stop. Then there'd be nothing but dead silence. Soon they'd continue walking a few more feet, before stopping again. Each time, a quick burst of light lit up the field and the surrounding area. They obviously were searching for those yellow eyes of a whitetail that might have wandered into the area.

Eventually, I observed the silhouettes of two men traveling side by side. I assumed one of them had the gun, while the other was operating the light. They were still a few yards away, coming directly toward me. My heart pounded wildly as the adrenaline rushed into my veins. I was afraid they'd hear my heart loudly beating, long before they reached my location.

I remained completely still, anxiously anticipating that moment to ambush them, hoping not to get shot in the process. Crunch, crunch, crunch. I heard the sounds of their feet crushing the frozen ground as they slowly approached. Again they stopped, briefly lighting up the back of the field. I thought to God they'd never reach my location. It sure would have been nice to have had a partner on this evening, but for some reason we would not be joining forces on this particular night.

I was out on my own! Crunch – crunch – crunch, they were getting closer. I remained completely motionless, tucked up against a tree along the edge of the field. I could see them slowly inching their way towards me. It was show and tell time. I jumped out of the woods, flashing my light directly on them, while at the same time screaming, "Game Warden, hold it right there!" You would've thought I'd painted raw turpentine on their bare butts, as they both screeched and shot off up across the field like launched rockets, scaring the hell out of me. I was close behind screaming as loud as I could for them to halt!

My demands for them to stop didn't slow them down one bit as they continued out across that field like a couple of race horses running full speed in the Kentucky Derby. They both realized there was a lot at stake for the both of them and that they needed to get out of there as soon as possible.

Smartly, they separated from each other, leaving me with no choice but to pursue the one closest to me. He was a big one, easily reaching 6 feet tall and he was built like a cement tower. I was amazed at how fast he was capable of running, especially considering his size. We shot out across the field and eventually onto the tarred Hemlock Hill Road itself.

I was gaining on him, which for me was a minor miracle in itself. I yelled, "If you don't stop, I'm going to have to shoot," hoping the threat of such an action would intimidate him enough into giving up, although I never intended to take such a drastic measure. Making that threat was a mistake. Instead of slowing down, he picked up speed, zig-zagging back and forth like a scared rabbit about to be pounced on by a wild coyote.

Finally, I got close enough to lunge for him, grabbing him around the neck. Down we went, rolling around into the ditch like a couple of tired-out pigs participating in a pig scramble at a country fair. I was completely out of breath, and so was he. I barely was capable of advising him that he was under arrest. I lay on top of him like a beached whale, pinning him to the ground. Neither of us could've gone much farther, nor did we have the strength to fight or struggle.

Regaining my composure, I managed to handcuff him. I was gasping between breaths while attempting to advise him of his constitutional rights. The right to remain silent and blah-blah-blah... He simply stated his name was Rodney and that he was from Bridgewater, Massachusetts. His driver's license confirmed this information. Other than that, Rodney refused to say who was with him, nor would he respond to any other questions I asked, as we slowly hiked back to the cruiser for the long, quiet ride to the Waldo County Jail.

"Rodney, I don't suppose you know a fellow by the name of Grover, do you?" I smartly inquired. I somehow suspected there might be some connection between the two, seeing that some of Grover's close relatives lived a short distance away from this location and my past experience revealed that many of Grover's hunting buddies came from the same Massachusetts area as Rodney.

"Grover! Grover, who? I ain't never heard of any gawd-damned Grover!" he sarcastically replied.

"I'm sure you haven't!" I smartly responded. Any further conversation between us at that point was basically over for the remainder of the long trip to Belfast. I quickly booked Rodney into the county facility charging him with the offense of night hunting, requesting for the jail to notify me if anyone showed up to post his bail.

Humorously, within a few hours of my departure, I received a radio message from the jail staff. "Warden Ford, your man was just freed on bail! A fellow by the name of Grover just arrived with plenty of cash to finalize the deal!" the dispatcher stated.

Surprise! Surprise! My hunch had been spot-on! Without a doubt, either Grover himself, or one of his nearby relatives, more than likely was accompanying Rodney that night out on

Hemlock Hill, but to prove it would be impossible. I think I'd have recognized Grover, had it been him.

Oh well, even though I didn't successfully capture the both of them, at least I'd finally bagged my first foot-jack-uh and another memory was placed into this warden's diary! Like so many times before, I'd simply wait to see what Grover's demeanor might be the next time we met. I'm sure he'd have something smart to say. Perhaps I'd recognize the subtle message of a scowl on his face followed by a single raised finger as we passed along the highway. But for some strange reason I liked the damned critter even though we were on opposite sides of the legal spectrum. For now, Grover wasn't the only night hunter prowling around in my district. It was time to find another spot to sit and wait, anticipating yet another adrenaline rush and perhaps another memory to be entered into the diaries.

I'll be Damned if I am Stopping for You
Every Time You Want

One of the most contentious and heated meetings between the two of us was in the fall of 1975. On that particular day, it was the last day of what had been a long hunting season. I was more than ready for the season to end, and a chance to get a little rest for a change. Needless to say, my temperament wasn't all that it could be. I was exhausted and short of patience to put it mildly.

On this day I had Jim Ross, the young warden recruit from Troy, riding with me. Jim had been a great help during my career, as he was actively pursuing a warden's career of his own. We were traveling on a dirt road in the town of Dixmont searching for hunters. Rumor had it that Grover and the gang were somewhere in the area. Just that fact alone was a good reason to be patrolling the area.

As we came to an intersection of the roads, I saw Grover's truck slowly coming my way. I said to Jim, "There's Grover and his buddies. I think I'll stop them and check to see if their guns are loaded and to make sure they have the proper licenses. I bet dollars to donuts, they are starting a deer drive or finishing one," I said to my buddy.

As they neared the intersection, I stepped out into the dirt road flagging them down. There were three men crowded into the cab of Grover's truck. We had just passed two or three other hunters a short distance back who seemed to be standing in one stationary location, making me wonder if perhaps there was a deer drive in the works. Grover came to a sudden and rather abrupt screeching halt, as I sauntered over to his truck asking to check their weapons and licenses. Before I could say anything more, Grover was out of the truck and on the fly, screaming obscenities and threats that could have been heard two towns away.

He was as boisterous and unruly as I'd ever seen him. "I'll be gawd-damned if I am going to be stopping for you every #*^# ing * %* you decide to jump out in front of me!" he yelled as he hurried across the road and started kicking the front of my cruiser. By now there were a few vehicles gathering behind us, unable to get by, as we had the road totally blocked. They were witnessing this mad outburst of tempers between the poacher and the lawman.

We both appeared as though we were trying to outdo each other, just seeing who could scream and yell the loudest. It had to have been a sight to behold for those hunters who were held up in traffic wondering what the hell they were witnessing. Grover was kicking the tires of my cruiser and likewise I was kicking at his truck. It was obvious neither one of us were making any headway with the insults and cuss words being thrown back and forth. It was only then that I realized what this loud distraction was being done for.

Grover's intention was to alert the hunters he'd left spread out along the road below, that the lawman was in the area. Everyone was for themselves! There were people who were on stands and the others getting ready to attempt the deer drive they planned to execute in that area. I had no violation on him and he knew it.

After a few minutes of continuous foul insanity, Grover jumped back into his truck, speeding out of the area, throwing gravel and rocks all over my cruiser in the process. I quickly spun the cruiser around, chasing the huge cloud of dust down the road. Poor Jim thought for sure that we were going to do battle. I wasn't so sure but what we were! "I noticed your carbine rifle laying on the back seat," Jim excitedly stated. "I didn't know but what I was going to have to load it and get it out there to you!" he nervously quipped.

As we sailed down the dusty road attempting to catch up with the truck, I noticed a young man diving behind a bunch of bushes in an attempt to hide as we headed his way. Slamming the brakes on, we skidded to an abrupt halt directly in front of where he lay. The hunter just happened to be one of Grover's sons who, unfortunately for him, didn't have a hunting license or the appropriate blaze orange hunting attire.

Normally, I would have considered simply writing out a summons for the violations, but due to the circumstances of this situation, I placed him under arrest, planning to haul him to the Waldo County Crowbar Hotel. A short distance away were a couple of other hunters, who appeared to be part of the group. They watched as we loaded Grover's son into the cruiser. Grover was screaming on ahead in a cloud of dust, trying to warn his crew to scatter out of the way because the law was in the area.

With my prisoner in the backseat, screaming his own volley of obscenities, we drove up to where these other men were standing. I recognized a couple of them from past experiences when I ran across Grover. Checking their licenses and having no issues with them, I calmly said, "When your buddy Grover comes back, you can tell him he's one short for the deer drive that was about to begin. His son will be at the Waldo County Jail waiting for someone to come bail him out!" I stated.

Neither of them made a comment as we headed out of the area destined for the county facility. That 1975 fall hunting season ended with one of our most contentious encounters thus far. I didn't know whether the coffee encounter we usually experienced after the hunting season passed, would happen this year or not. But it did! We had the usual banter back and forth in a jovial sort of way. His only comment regarding our Dixmont temper tantrums was something to the effect of "that was quite a show we put on for those hunters waiting for us to clear the road wasn't it? You didn't have to be so rough on the boy though!" he chuckled.

225

And this was the way our two careers seemingly went – the many hunting seasons with the usual confrontations of one kind or another, always ending with a sign of mutual respect. It was that relationship between the game warden and Grover that certainly made him the most memorable of the characters I had dealt with.

Retirement, a New Career, and the Book

By the late 1980s, it was obvious the fish and wildlife agency was rapidly changing. The job I once loved no longer was the dream I'd envisioned. The department had gone to shift work. We were told when to work and where. In addition, we had been placed on mileage restrictions in order to keep the operating costs of the agency within their allotted budget. Restrictions that proved to hinder our enforcement efforts. Those of us who ignored these new rules and kept on answering our complaints from the public as we'd been so accustomed to, suddenly found ourselves being reprimanded.

The mileage allotments and the assigned hours we were allowed to work no longer met the needs of protecting the wildlife and serving the public as in the past. I found myself constantly being called on the carpet and disciplined for doing the job I'd been hired to do back in 1970. I suddenly realized that *living the dream* had turned into what I considered to be more like *living a nightmare.*

It definitely was my time to move on. I couldn't blame our department, or my bosses, for these new changes in operations. Most of the changes were dictated by the Federal Government, the labor relations boards and the bargaining demands of our own union – not to mention the high costs of maintaining the agency. Management within our agency was simply following the many demands of a changing society. The department could ill afford to pay overtime for the number of hours that we were working as we had in the past. Overtime we never asked for, nor did we expect! I knew the more I resisted, the closer I was creeping into either being dumped into a forced retirement, or even worse, being fired.

I was my own worst enemy when it came to fighting for what I considered to be the great career I had chosen. Being vocal and disobedient was my own doing, and without a doubt it was close to becoming my own demise. I simply couldn't adjust to the many new operational changes and therefore I knew it was my time to bring a closure to *living the dream* while I still could. I decided to retire in 1990 in order to make a political run for the office of High Sheriff in our county. My good friend, Stanley Knox, was retiring from the position after 20 years of being the county's top law enforcement officer. Stan was leaving law enforcement after having served 20 years with the State Police, another 20 years as Waldo County's High Sheriff, and a few years as a Chief of Police in a southern Maine town. He had served the citizens well. But he too knew when it was time to move along.

So in early 1990, I announced my retirement and the plans to politically seek the Sheriff's position – a decision that was not only good for the department, but for me personally. Humorously, a good friend, former local State Representative Ken "Babe" Tozier, agreed to become my campaign treasurer. "Babe" as we called him, was remotely related to Grover through marriage. During one of the campaign stops at a local restaurant, Grover was having lunch. Babe sauntered over his way, inquiring if he'd make a donation toward my Sheriff's campaign. Grover stated, "I'd be glad to donate," as he reached into his pocket pulling out a thin dime. Handing it to Babe with a huge smirk on his face he said, "I hope this helps!"

He then burst out laughing in that loud chuckle that we both had become so accustomed to. Fortunately, I won that election and took over the title as Waldo County's Top Cop! The job was a complete turn-around compared to what I'd been accustomed to doing. I now had all of patrol, the jail, and civil process to operate. It was a new challenge to say the least. It was a bit overwhelming to begin with. And just like what the Fish and Game Department had gone through mandate-wise, so too was all of law enforcement.

Suddenly, here I was, trying to run an agency under the same guidelines that I so bitterly detested when I was a warden. As time passed and after two four-year terms as Sheriff, I decided to write books and travel around the countryside relating the many adventures I'd experienced as a game warden.

Again, thanks to the wise advice of my stepfather, Retired Warden Verne Walker, who suggested I keep the diaries and maybe one day write that book. I thought it only fair to tell the stories as they really happened and to be as truthful as possible.

One day, as I was riding along in the department's cruiser, I happened to come up behind Grover as he was traveling to unknown territories. I pulled him over, wanting to inquire if he had any issues with my writing books and telling his story as well as mine. As usual, as he sat on the edge of the busy highway, the response was, "What the hell are you pulling me over for now?"

I'll never forget that smirk on his face when I told him of my intentions. He proudly responded, "Go ahead. By all means. Just tell it like it was!" he chuckled to himself in that typical Grover mannerism. Long after the books were published, retired state trooper, Mark Nickerson, and I were traveling around the countryside sharing our experiences and promoting them.

One of those evenings we had what I considered an interesting engagement at the Waterville Elks Club. There were close to 300 people in the audience, one of them being Grover and some of his family. Grover's name came up during the event because of his notoriety in the area. To the delight of the audience I humorously began sharing some of our more interesting moments with the group, much to the pleasure of my old poaching buddy and his family.

After the event, I was signing and selling books when Grover and his daughter came up and stood alongside of the table. Together we started all over again sharing a laugh or two. People would purchase my books, politely asking for a signature. Then they would approach Grover asking him to sign. I had to tell them, "Now those are what you might call, some real collectibles!" And they were! The photo below of Grover, his daughter, and the lawman, is a friendly reminder of that evening.

Sharing laughs with the notorious Grover. We had developed a mutual respect for one another despite a few knock down, dragouts over the years. A sign that peace can truly be accomplished.

A few of the wild critters to come through the warden's menagerie

Just like my mother's many days of caring for wild animals, there were a few times when as a district game warden I inherited a few wildlife critters of my own to care for. I'll share a few of those memories during that era. Memories that made my warden's career a little more exciting and enjoyable. For example, there was "Cheerio," a small partridge that was brought to my sanctuary by a well-meaning sportsman who had plucked it out of the roadway before it was struck and killed by a passing motorist. Cheerio was an appropriate name for the upland game bird, seeing as where most of the time it perched on the back of my living room couch at the Burnham warden's camp, waiting for me to feed it the small circular bits of cereal,

one bit at a time. Cheerio loved the small circular cereal bits and thus it was only appropriate to name the bird after its favorite food.

Cheerio was as tame as any wild creature I'd ever had. She wanted to be at my side no matter where I was, or what I was doing. When we were outside, she'd ride upon the hood of my riding lawn mower as I went 'round and 'round in the yard. Or whenever I was outside taking a break, she'd find a spot next to where I was sitting, making sure to remain as close as possible by following my every move.

Then one late summer day, Cheerio disappeared never to be seen again. I only hoped she had hooked up with another bird of her own species, where together they'd wandered back out into the wilderness where they truly belonged. I was left with a dilemma of sorts on what to do with all those extra boxes of Cheerios I had stocked up on, though. Say what you want, but some of these wild animals have a means of creating a personal bond with certain humans. Cheerio happened to have been one of them. Over the years I heard of others who had been befriended by a partridge, especially men who spent their careers working in the woods for a living. I felt as though during Cheerio's stay at my warden's camp I too had that special bond with a partridge, about like the one I had with Fritzi the fisher, back in the earlier days of my youth.

Wiley, the Foxy Little Coyote

"Hello, are you the area's game warden?" a young lady inquired when I answered the phone. I couldn't help but wonder if this was another one of those phone calls that left me pondering whether I should admit to my profession or not. "I am," I reluctantly responded. "What can I help you with?"

"Well sir, our cat just came back from being out in the woods behind our house. She was toting a little ball of gray fur in her mouth. I think it's a baby coyote, she stated. We've been hearing them out back for quite some time now," she excitedly sputtered. "Could you please come pick it up? Its eyes aren't even open and it's barely moving. I just don't know what to do with it?" she pleaded.

I couldn't help thinking, "Mmmmm, another of those damned wild animal complaints. One where some poor little critter has been needlessly plucked away from its mother." At the same time, the idea of raising a baby coyote sounded a bit exciting.

"I'll be right over to take him off your hands, ma'am," I politely responded, all the while I was trying to hide my enthusiasm about possibly raising a young coyote. In no time I was holding a small dark-gray creature inside the palm of my hand. Like the complainant stated, it was alive, but just barely moving, as I quickly scanned it looking for any possible damages inflicted by the cat. Seeing none, I placed the little critter into a small cardboard box and a towel for him to snuggle into during the transport back home.

Back at home, I prepared a larger cardboard box lined with cloth and two larger hot water bottles wrapped tightly in cotton towels. The heat from the bottle caused the little tyke to snuggle up as close to the warmth as he could get. Without a doubt, he probably assumed his momma had returned. This cardboard box would become his new home for the time being.

I quickly determined this newest addition to our family to be a young male. Appropriately, believing him to be a coyote, I decided to call him Wiley. Gathering up a collection of small baby bottles I'd used in past rehabilitation efforts, I proceeded to fill them with a delicate mixture of warm evaporated milk, water, and a little touch of kaopectate to control diarrhea. I then commenced giving Wiley his first official feeding away from home. The little bugger was rather hungry as he quickly caught onto the feeding habits which hopefully were going to keep him alive.

That next day I headed to Augusta, seeking a written permit from the department to raise what, at this time, was considered to be a highly controversial animal by the sportsmen in our state. To put it mildly, coyotes certainly were not the most favorable of creatures roaming through our woodlands by many citizens. Many sportsmen, if given the chance, would eradicate every one of them. Meeting with the Chief Warden, Larry Cummings, he quickly typed up and authorized the rehab permit to raise Wiley. "A coyote huh? That should be an interesting critter to raise John. Please be sure to let me know how he's doing," Larry said, as he signed the legal document authorizing me to keep the small critter.

Word spread quickly throughout the area that I was raising a baby coyote. Several rather inquisitive sportsmen stopped by our home for a peek of the little creature. All of them left the area stating what a handsome little tyke he was. Wiley grew rapidly, as his daily consumption of warm milk seemingly increased with every meal. Slowly his brown eyes opened, affording Wiley the chance to observe the big world around him for the very first time. By now he had developed a little personality of his own, as he scooted around inside the cardboard box whenever one of us approached.

After a few weeks of feeding and caring for Wiley, I began noticing a rather strange change in his appearance. His dark gray coating suddenly was beginning to turn much lighter in color and a lot redder than what I expected of a coyote. Strangely something very different appeared to be happening to his tail. There was a little white tip forming on the very end of it. Suddenly, I knew my dreams of raising a coyote were about to change drastically. Wiley, was transgressing from what I thought was a mean old coyote into a handsome little red fox. Oh boy! Now what was I going to tell all those folks who assumed I was raising a coyote? How is it possible for the local game warden, a warden who had gone so far as to obtain a department permit to raise a wild coyote, to make such a drastic mistake?

Wiley was quickly turning into a handsome red fox. How was I ever going to explain this error of wildlife mis-identification to those who had already seen Wiley? After all, wasn't the game warden supposed to be the expert on these types of wild animals! Oh well, it would have to be what it would be. Hopefully I was prepared for the harassing that was sure to come, and one which I rightfully deserved.

Wiley continued growing at a rapid rate. In no time, he was displaying a handsome red coat and a big bushy tail. A tail with a bright white tip on the very end. He was extremely playful, as he freely roamed throughout our house as if he were a small puppy. He definitely was right at home, even to the point of being potty trained.

Wiley had a habit of following us wherever we went, constantly looking for someone to play with or for someone to scratch his head and back. It was hard to refuse his efforts, especially after looking into those handsome brown eyes. Little Wiley grew up accepting and trusting the presence of anyone who happened to stop by for a visit. He even regarded total strangers as if they were his best friend. Living with Wiley roaming throughout the house was like having a young puppy around. He'd curl up by my feet or he would lay sprawled out in my lap at night as I watched television. Wherever I went, he was quick to follow behind, closely hanging onto my every footstep.

Little John sharing a precious moment with Wiley

In essence, our furry little friend had turned into a loving member of the family. As the summer progressed, Wiley continued growing. I determined it was about time to put him outdoors where I hoped he'd eventually return back to the wild where he belonged. Wiley quickly established himself out in the thick woods behind our house, but it certainly didn't deter him from having a desire to be constantly around people who came to visit.

His long list of trusted friends grew with every stranger who entered the yard. Whenever we were outside, he'd come running out of the woods looking for a handout of grub, or he'd grab onto some article of interest that caught his eye. He stole more than one item out of the yard, hauling them off into the woods to hide. I recall a time when he grabbed one of Little John's brand new sneakers, running down into the woods where he buried it deep in the brush. We spent two days looking for the new sneaker before finally spotting it hidden in among some stumps and thick bushes. God forbid if I left a pack of cigarettes lying around. He'd snatch them up in a heartbeat, running off into the woods with them firmly secured between his sharp little teeth. I'd never see them again. I knew he wasn't smoking or eating them. Perhaps in a subtle kind of way, he was trying to tell me something I should have known.

Most every evening at around supper time, Wiley exited the woods headed for the house. He'd stand in front of our kitchen window waiting for us to pay attention to him, obviously seeking a handout of grub! If we ignored him, he'd lunge feet first against the glass windows, making us aware of his presence. It was this type of action, that scared the bejeezus out of more than one unsuspecting visitor, as we all sat around our kitchen table chatting.

Wiley eventually turned into a handsome mature fox, with a beautiful coat of shiny bright-red fur. He was easily identified by the white tip on the end of his tail. One day near the end of summer, I met up with Chief Warden Cummings during my travels. Immediately he inquired, "Hey John, how's that coyote you're raising doing?"

Telling a little fib of sorts, I sheepishly responded, "Oh my coyote died Larry, but did I tell you about the little red fox I'm raising?" I sheepishly responded. I'm sure he knew the difference, as he simply grinned and graciously walked away! I'd been taking an awful razzing from most everybody who knew the real story, somehow I suspected Larry knew the difference. But being the real gentleman and the pro that he was, he was going to spare me the grief I already was getting.

With the arrival of the cool fall weather, Wiley's trips to the house were becoming less frequent. It was obvious that he was transgressing back into the wilderness where he belonged. It seemed as if he was straying farther and farther away from home.

One day the phone rang once again. "Hi John, this is your neighbor up the road! I just had something very strange happen in my dooryard," he excitedly exclaimed. "I had a fox out in our driveway that came running right up to us. I think it might be rabid, so I shot it. What should I do with the carcass?" he inquired.

I felt a huge lump rise in my throat and my eyes watered up as I informed him to simply discard the carcass. I explained to him as best I could under the conditions, how I was quite sure the animal he had just killed was my little Wiley. I don't know who felt the worst, me or him. I certainly couldn't fault him for his actions. His concerns were genuine. The discussions concerning rabies in our area had been widely publicized over the years and thus everybody was very leery of any wild animal wandering right up to them, as they very well should have been.

The last picture of Wiley before he was gone

Sadly, my neighbor had no idea that I'd nurtured Wiley from his earlier days. On the other hand, I couldn't force myself to retrieve the carcass, disposing of it as I normally would have done without hesitation. Without protesting my serious lack of enthusiasm to assist him in disposing of the carcass, humbly my neighbor apologized, stating that he understood. He agreed he'd take care of it on his own. For the next several days, I found myself scanning the woods behind our house, hoping to see that magnificent little critter coming through the bushes just one more time. But sadly, it wasn't meant to be!

At least I had some fond memories and a few pictures of my little buddy Wiley, reminding me of those good old days and the happy memories the little pet brought to our family. This story was yet another cherished memory included in my warden diaries. I only wish it had been a story with a much happier ending.

One late winter morning, just as I was munching on my breakfast while planning on enjoying a day off from the regular patrolling routine, the telephone rang. One thing about the warden's job, folks never knew whether we were on a day off or not. The phone had a means of keeping us constantly in contact. The phone ringing around our place was quite normal. Our home phone numbers were made readily available to the public we served. Answering it was considered a part of our official duties. Unlike today, where it sometimes is hard to get a chance to even speak to a warden without going through several hoops in the process. The phone was a requirement of the profession in order for us to be able to answer the public's needs and inquiries.

"Are you the area's district game warden?" the lady excitedly inquired.

"I am!" I politely responded. "What can I help you with?" I asked.

"This is the Dixmont Corner Store. We've got a little dilemma up here that requires your expert advice," she anxiously stated. "A woodcutter is here with two owl eggs that fell out of a tree he was cutting down this morning. The mother owl kept dive-bombing him, but there's no way he can put the eggs back into the fallen tree," she stated. "This poor woodcutter feels terrible, and hopes something can be done to save them," she further explained. "These eggs appear to be okay, without any cracks or defects. We are just wondering what we should do with them?" she nervously inquired.

"Good question," I mumbled. "I doubt if they'll hatch, but I suggest wrapping them in something soft and placing them in a real warm spot where they'll be left undisturbed," I advised her. "I'm on day off and I won't be able to pick them up today, but I'll come by the first thing tomorrow morning to get them,"

I rather disgustedly sputtered. I figured it was going to be a waste of time trying to do anything with these eggs, but by at least making the effort to these folks believing that I was doing something with them, was good public relations if nothing else. I'd simply go to the store, gather them up, planning to discard them later on when no one was around. Who knows, maybe I'd scale them out the cruiser window on the way back home and no one would ever be the wiser. The chances of these eggs hatching was remote at best. But I knew that if I suggested simply destroying them to the people at the store, the repercussions from those who felt they were helping out Mother Nature could be brutal. I'd certainly seen that picture before!

"Okay, thank you ever so much," she said. "We'll wrap them up in cotton and place them on top of the popcorn machine in the store," she excitedly exclaimed. With a resolution to the problem being made, we ended the conversation. At the conclusion of our phone conversation I made a little note to myself, "pick up the eggs at the Dixmont store" for my things to do early the next morning.

I'd forgotten all about that previous call, when early the next morning the phone rang again. "John, this is the Dixmont Store again. You aren't going to believe this, but we did exactly as you told us and we've just watched one of the eggs hatching!" she excitedly sputtered. "I think the other one is about ready to hatch too," she gushed.

"You're, kidding me," I responded in total disbelief. "I'll be along soon to get them," I promised. All the while I was thinking, "Now what the hell am I going to do?" And thus my adventure of becoming momma to a pair of young owlets began. Little did I realize it at the time, but what an exciting adventure it would become with a whole host of challenges.

Gathering up the small box containing the homeliest creatures God had ever created, I brought the young owls home. Inside the small box of cotton were two little pink gobs of meat that looked like small balls of slimy raw hamburg. They had no feathers, as they just lay there. Their eyes were yet to open, instead there were little blobs of purple skin where their eyes were located. They were by far the ugliest looking critters I'd ever seen. It looked as though God had been busy making them, when all of a sudden he decided he was all done for the day, never bothering to finish the product!

Once back home, I placed a distress call to Birds Acres, a non-profit rehabilitation group in Ellsworth, asking them for some form of "owl parental" guidance. "Don't get your hopes up that they'll survive," I was bluntly told. "They need mice, squirrels, and other foods from the wild to survive," I was informed. "You'll need to chop these carcasses up into fine pieces, making sure to leave the hair and bones intact," the expert on the other end of the phone, calmly stated.

I thought to myself, "Oh that's just great, I don't think I can go to the local supermarket and buy a package of dead mice, squirrels, or other furry wild critters!" This project already was off to a very bleak and unpromising beginning as far as I was concerned. For the time being, I quickly prepared their new nest out of the usual den material, a cardboard box. I then began filling warm water bottles wrapped in towels for heat and placed a cloth lining in the bottom of the box for them to snuggle into.

I then managed to somehow get a little raw hamburg into them, which was quite a surprise in itself. I'd tickle their little beaks, with the hamburg firmly held together with tweezers, which apparently they thought was mom coming to the nest with a bit of chow. Once they opened their mouths, I quickly dropped the raw hamburg inside, which they seemed to swallow in one or two quick gulps. Hopefully the meal of raw hamburg would keep them alive until such time that I could get my hands on the real food that they so desperately needed – the kind of meal with hair, bones, and raw meat included on the menu! I immediately sent out a distress call within the neighborhood for anyone who had an extra supply of dead mice, rats, squirrels, or any other forms of dead critter that would make great owl feed in their yards, to please rally around my cause by delivering their stash to our house. "Simply leave them on the doorstep if we aren't there," was the final instructions I gave to those who were offering to help.

In the meantime, I suddenly found myself patrolling the highway, desperately searching for any dead critter that had fallen victim to a speeding motorist. I was like a crow searching the pavement for a spattered creature who had fallen victim to a speeding vehicle. Upon locating a road casualty such as a squirrel, woodchuck, or even a raccoon, I'd quickly exit the cruiser grabbing the dead carcass to salvage as future "owl food." I really was like that crow, cruising the pavement looking for a quick meal.

Arriving back home with my cache, I grabbed a trusty pair of tinsnips as I became a wildlife butcher of sorts, chopping up whatever furry critter was on the chopping block. Placing the small chunks of meat, hair, and small bones, into several small plastic tubs, the food supply was starting to come together. Amazingly my many neighbors and friends were rallying to the cause. People were dropping off dead mice, squirrels, and even woodchucks on our doorstep in an effort to provide an ample supply of feed for the owlets.

All of this gruesome activity certainly didn't make Mrs. Ford any too happy. Especially when I placed some of the plastic tubs in the refrigerator to keep them from spoiling. She never knew what dead creature would be draped across our doorstep from one day to the next. I spent countless hours snipping away at these dead carcasses, storing the gruesome remains in little plastic tubs for future use. That tender loving "owl care" required a drastic change in my daily patrol routine. I found myself heading home every few hours to change the hot water bottles and to force feed the babies I now was playing the roll of mama to.

They staggered around in their little cardboard box, as content as if they were high in a tree in amongst a wooden nest.

As they stood in the bottom of the cardboard box they were only a few inches tall. These owlets had big feet, large bulging unopened eyes, huge beaks, and no feathers covering their fragile bodies. They were extremely ugly in their overall appearance. Their appearance was certainly a look that only a mother could appreciate! As I brushed the small chunks of furry meat from the remains of dead mice and the other critters across their beaks, they gobbled the goodies down like they were getting a feed of candy. There was no chewing of the food. Instead it all disappeared down their gullet in one swift swallow, as they continued begging for more.

Amazingly, these homely little creatures grew quite rapidly. They constantly demanded more food and care. Within a few days, a layer of white downy feathers had completely encased their bodies as their bluish-gray eyes had finally opened, giving them a little character for a change. They meandered around in their small nest of warm water bottles anxiously waiting for yet another hand-out of hair, bones, and meat. The trips from patrolling to back home for these feeding frenzies were becoming more frequent. I found myself becoming quite attached to the owlets. I named them Who-Who and Boo-Hoo! As if I could honestly tell the difference between either of them!

Fortunately, they'd made it through those first few hectic days. Now I had high hopes that they'd survive. It almost seemed as if God had come back to work, as each day the changes in appearance was quite evident.

This must have been the year for abandoned owlets. Shortly after inheriting these wild creatures, I'd called my wildlife rehab mother informing her of the great undertaking I was now going through, only to have her say, "Well I'm doing better than you. I have three of my own that I'm raising!" she boasted. Eventually she sent along a photo of her own prized works.

Mother had three barred owlets at the menagerie she was raising

I could tell that our little owlets were progressing just as well as hers, in size and appearance. They all looked as if they had come from the same nest. The little owlets meandered around in their small nest of warm water bottles, anxiously waiting for yet another handout of hair, bones, and meat.

Fortunately, they'd made it through those first few hectic days and now I hoped they'd survive. The daily routine of constant feeding continued throughout the summer. Miraculously, they were quickly turning into masterpieces of sheer beauty. Their downy feathers were replaced with gray and brown feathers as their bodies increased in size to that of maturity. The small box that was their nest, had to be replaced with a larger one providing more room.

The daily feedings required a lot more food. Thank God the highway was producing its share of road-killed squirrels, woodchucks, and other creatures to snip apart for future meals. Who-Who and Boo-Hoo lived upstairs in our home right along with the Ford family until one evening as we were watching TV, one of them came staggering into the living room. Somehow they'd discovered a means of escaping from the box that, up until then, had been their nest and now they were exploring the big world around them.

Mrs. Ford gruffly demanded an immediate end to their ability to roam freely about the house. "They'll be sh***ing all over everything, John," she stated in that authoritative tone of voice I fully understood. There was to be no compromising with the Queen of the household, allowing them to remain upstairs, that was for sure. Who-Who and Boo-Hoo were quickly transferred into a portion of our cellar in an area where they could roam about as they pleased. Their new home afforded them an open view of the woods behind our home that would eventually become their own.

I had covered the cellar door over with chicken wire, providing them with a "birds-eye" view of the woods and ground outside. No pun intended! Their daily diet changed from whole mice to chicken necks that I found myself purchasing in bulk at a chicken processing plant in nearby Belfast. They learned how to fly on their own, spending most of the time perched on a beam overlooking the wilderness outdoors.

As fall approached, the time for freedom was close at hand. Who-Who and Boo-Hoo by now were a pair of handsome, mature Barred Owls, a far cry from that first day when I brought the ugly little creatures home. The final challenge I was facing was teaching them how to survive on their own. I wanted to be sure they were capable of hunting down food that would allow them to exist.

The natural instinct in performing such a task was obviously present as I watched them from afar, but to satisfy my own mind I secured large chunks of cut-up squirrel meat and loosely attached by the hairs to a length of monofilament fishing line. I would toss the meat up at the other end of my cellar, rapidly dragging the meal across the floor, in plain view of the owlets as they sat on their perch overhead. Their heads bobbed up and down as they intently watched their supper scooting along the floor in front of them. After a few attempts, they soon discovered how to fly down from their perch and strike at the moving target, devouring the moving meal. It wasn't until I pulled the meat rapidly back across the floor that they were capable of striking at it in that one swift move. Prior to that, they realized that if they simply landed and stood in the direction the meal was coming, all they had to do was reach down and pick it up as it slowly passed on by.

The process at that point, kind of reminded me as if I was making a delivery of "meals on wheels" to the pair. Thus the quick toss and retrieve brought them to the point of where they had to attack it if they wanted to eat! They quickly mastered the art.

The time had come to release them back into the wilderness where they belonged. Late one September afternoon, I removed the wire barrier from the cellar door, allowing them to freely move outside when they were ready. It took them awhile but eventually they worked their way outdoors and into freedom, perching in a nearby tree at the end of our porch, where they both fell asleep.

At dusk, they moved up onto the TV antennae on my roof, where once again they dozed off for another nap.

Little John sharing a photo op with one of the barred owls

The owls huddled together atop the roof, nearly caused a major traffic jam with folks traveling through the area. More than one excited motorist skidded into the dooryard screaming, "Come outside and see what the hell is perched on your TV antennae!" Papa Owl was quite proud of his accomplishments. I explained the circumstances surrounding the rare sight to those strangers and friends who stopped for a closer look.

By the next morning they were gone. The next day I called out to them, hoping they'd respond at least one more time. It was only then that I realized what the old saying of, "having the kids leave the nest," really meant. I already missed them. Suddenly, from out of the trees they flew, landing a few feet from where I stood. Their heads were bobbing up and down as they anxiously looked for yet another handout of free grub from Dad.

In the following days, the visits became less frequent until finally they disappeared for good. I hoped they would celebrate the life they were destined for. They had survived some rather unusual circumstances.

The phone rang once again. "Hello, are you the game warden?" a lady's voice inquired.

"I am, Ma'am, what can I help you with?

"We found a baby woodchuck in our driveway and don't know what to do with it, do you have any suggestions?"

Here we go again! I could hardly wait. And so it went, we never knew what wild critter would be the next to come through the door, just like it did back in those early days of living at the menagerie back home.

Karma Finally Returned After a Long Period of Time

What is the meaning of karma? Karma refers to "What goes around, comes around." Or "You reap what you sow." and "For every action there is an equal and opposite reaction." These are the everyday phrases, cliches even, that actually describe it the best.

I wanted to finish my stories by going back to the earlier part of this book, at a time when I was starting my young career and had expressed the frustration I'd experienced dealing in a compromising situation with a trapper named Jimbo.

Jimbo managed to take advantage of my inexperience and humiliated this new warden who was just starting his career and I foolishly allowed it to happen because of my own stupidity! In reality, today I should thank him for placing me into that life-learning experience – having been so easily hoodwinked in the lessons of trapping and how the trappers operated.

I had to admit, it was a sport in which I had little, if any, knowledge. But because of that humiliating lesson, I was determined to get educated just as quickly as possible into the many habits, techniques, and the artful knowledge of trapping by these people. I wanted to be prepared for the future and to never again fall victim to my own stupidity, although that thought was nothing more than a pipe dream at best. I was sure there'd be many other humiliating and embarrassing times over my career. And there certainly were!

But as I rushed into becoming educated in the art of trapping as best I could, there were a few violators who, once they realized why I had come after them with a vengeance, they could personally thank Jimbo for making the learning process possible. I recalled those wise words of my stepfather, Verne

Walker, and Retired Warden Milton Scribner, that "What goes around, comes around."

"Time is on your side, file away those issues that got you here and who was pulling the wool over your eyes. If indeed they are real poachers and if they remain active, rest assured their day of reckoning will come," they advised. "There'll be a time of reckoning when you can get what we called "a little payback!"

Both men were right. I had Jimbo's two incidents filed away on the back burner, anxiously anticipating that day when karma would come around. After all, he had seized advantage of me once, at a time when I so foolishly bought into his alibi that he was recovering a trap he had lost the previous year. But then, he was enjoying his devious trickery so much, that he tried once again, when I tagged his furs that year. Fool me once, shame on me! Fool me twice and shame on you!

Although our paths never crossed nearly as often as I thought they might, I was still hearing from credible sources that Jimbo was still very much a snake, fish and game wise, as he'd been that first time we met.

Finally in November of 1985, I was tipped off about a little-known hunting practice Jimbo had been performing for years. During the hunting season Jimbo always managed to end up with a big buck to tag, trying to make those who knew him well think that he was some type of a great white hunter.

According to the informant, once Jimbo tagged out and legally registered his deer, he'd sneak down into the back field behind his farm, where he'd continue hunting and shooting deer for others in his crowd and family to tag. Supposedly this activity was often accomplished under the cover of darkness and beneath a bright light being cast out into the grazing deer's eyes.

"He has a rather elaborate tree stand down there," my informant boldly stated. Armed with this knowledge, I grabbed my faithful deputy and together we went on a scouting mission. Accompanied by Deputy Warden, Scott Sienkiewicz, we scouted the area behind his house, familiarizing ourselves with the layout of the land for future reference. Sure enough, midway out in the backfield, located along the edge of the woods, was an elaborate blind complete with a roof, sliding windows, and a comfortable easy chair.

The blind provided him with a perfect view of the entire field. The place was exactly what the informant stated it would be. I decided one of my main missions for this fall's hunting activity was to give this newly-acquired information the work it deserved. "If you catch him, the entire area around here would be tickled to death!" the informant chuckled. "He thinks you are somewhat afraid of the dark, and that you'd never be the wiser to his elaborate plan!" he stated.

I carefully watched the tagging books in the store where Jimbo usually tagged his deer, just waiting for him to bring his usual big buck in. It wasn't long into the season before Jimbo actually did tag out. I assumed from that point on, he'd be using the tree stand directly behind his farm – that sacred place where he felt safe and secure.

As luck had it, that very first attempt we made into the area, found us hiking a fair distance through the woods in order to get to the back field. There was roughly a half hour of legal hunting time to go before sunset and the time when all hunting ceased. I depended upon using whatever light was left to get us into position, not knowing if he would be there or if he might be coming into the area later. We were prepared to spend some time waiting, even if it meant returning several nights later.

By the time we reached the location, it was close to darkness. The legal shooting hours for the day had ended. Sliding in behind the tree stand, it appeared as if no one was there. I advised Scott, "I'm going up the ladder to see if he's been here or even if he has been using it," I stated. I slowly maneuvered up the homemade ladder to the back door of the tree hut. Stepping inside I was looking for signs that it was being used, when by chance I happened to look up across the field in the direction of where the farm was located. Low and behold, Jimbo was just now hiking down into the area on foot.

I bailed out of the tree house never using the ladder. I almost landed on Scotty's head, nearly scaring him to death. "He's just now coming down into the area! We'll let him get into place and wait him out!" I advised Scott. "We'll just hide underneath these hemlock branches, waiting and watching. Who knows, maybe he'll blister another deer and make our efforts all the more worthwhile," I snickered.

Jimbo, none the wiser that we were within a few feet of his location, slowly climbed the ladder, grasping the high-powered rifle firmly in his hand. We heard him settling down inside the blind and then for a long period of time there was nothing but a dead silence.

After a while, a brief sweep of the field was made by a bright beam of light coming from the flashlight Jimbo was toting. Our night hunting case was complete, but I chose to wait until he came down from the blind before making our presence known. More time passed, and then there was yet another sweep of light. But no deer had come into the green field. Finally, much later in the evening and after one last sweep of the field with the beam of light, we could hear rustling coming from inside the blind. Soon the door opened, and Jimbo slowly started backing down the ladder, preparing to call it a night.

It was show and tell time, as we both quickly surrounded the sight with Jimbo firmly latched onto the ladder. "Doing a little late hunting are you, Jimbo?" I yelled, as I cast the beam of my flashlight directly onto him. The moment was priceless, he appeared to be totally in a mild state of shock and couldn't move. He was frozen to the ladder. I had to climb up on it, prying the loaded firearm out of his cold hands.

Karma had finally returned after all those years, he experienced the humiliation I'd received 15 years before from the many friends Jimbo thought he had. The ones who he'd openly bragged about how he had pulled the wool over the stupid, new and naive warden's eyes!

It was a priceless payback moment in time, when karma had finally returned! Jimbo was charged with night hunting, hunting deer after already killing one, his rifle was seized for evidence, and eventually his licenses with the agency were suspended. Jimbo ended up paying a hefty fine in the end.

My informant was exactly right. The complimentary calls I received from those many buddies of Jimbo's, and even some from a few of his enemies, made this concentrated effort well worthwhile. Life indeed was being good.

As I left that area of woods on that cool and frosty night, I couldn't help thinking, "You know, in so many ways, I really was *living the dream* and what a dream it had been!

Then and Now

As my warden's career came to an end, I couldn't help but thank God for the great career it had been. I was blessed in so many ways, especially to have been hired at the time I was. And to have been assigned to a district that provided so many great memories, and lived the dream during that era when I loved every minute of what I was doing, was the best.

As I joined the force in 1970, several of the older wardens, Verne Walker, Milton Scribner, Reggie Mosey, Leon and Murray Gilpatrick, and a whole slew of others, were just ending their careers. They all claimed to have lived through the best of times. The new operational changes that were being forced upon them were a bit more than they cared to deal with.

Changes such as the dog leash laws, the boating laws, the beginning of the snowmobile enforcement and the littering enforcement, were all areas of discontent that they felt was taking away from their main goal of protecting the wildlife.

But as they rode off into the sunset, not one of them expressed any regrets for the great careers they too had experienced. "It's time to let the new generation take over and deal with these new changes," they agreed.

As a young recruit just starting out in the business, I didn't know the difference. After all, I was beginning to live my own dream, and I was doing it at a time when I regarded the job as being the best profession around.

Now at the end of my tour, and after going through so many new changes in our own working procedures, shift work being the worst, I knew exactly how those older gentlemen had felt. I suddenly found myself thinking exactly as they did, "It was time to move on and let the newer generation take over!"

I guess that happens within any profession, whether you are working for the public or whatever career it was. Society constantly changes, attitudes change, operational procedures change, and the entire warden profession itself had moved into a new era of time. The young folks, replacing us older troops, were seeking their own dreams. They have that same burning desire and heightened enthusiasm that we too experienced back in our days.

Today's training is much more professional, the issued equipment of today is far better than anything we ever could have imagined. There were no cell phones, computers, game cameras, pagers, night scopes, airboats, jet skis, high-powered snowmobiles, ATVs, GPSs, and the list goes on.

We survived our careers simply with the very basics, but we made do with what we had. Even in our times, we had more than our predecessors did. The 120 wardens who were in the field when I joined, all have their own great stories and tales to tell. Many of them are far better than anything I have shared.

Every one of my cohorts loved the profession we chose. For us it wasn't just a job, but instead, it was a way of life. Our lives! We were a strong brotherhood, consisting of different personalities and ideals. But all of us were devoted to caring for the wildlife we protected and serving the sportsmen who paid our wages. Just like those young wardens who have replaced us today, their primary duties are working for the sportsmen and protecting the natural resources. Their futures, and those of the department, depend upon providing the public with the very best services possible.

Since 1880, fifteen warden service members paid the ultimate price – sacrificing their lives while performing their official duties. Four of those on the list were personal friends. May they rest in peace knowing that their memories will never be forgotten.

In closing I wish to dedicate this book to all of the wardens from the past, those of the present, and to those who will come along in the future.

"Living the dream" is exactly what it's all about. May each of you get to live your own dreams.

CPSIA information can be obtained
at www.ICGtesting.com
Printed in the USA
LVHW052118121219
640325LV00002B/99/P